FISHING STORIES

by Bob Becker

Adventures on Lakes and Streams

Printed 1994
In the United States of America
by WHITE BIRCH PRINTING, INC.
Spooner, Wisconsin 54801

Second Printing, 1994
Third Printing, 1995
Fourth Printing, 1997
Fifth Printing, 1998

ISBN 1-885548-02-8

To order, contact:
BOOT PRINTS
701 College St.
Spooner, WI 54801
Phone (715) 635-2317

Dedication

To Marian.....my best catch of all!

Foreword

A time once existed in my life when a penny fish hook was a priceless possession. With one, a couple yards of white "store string" from the butcher shop, and a slender willow stick, I'd be in fishing heaven as I trudged across the fields of my grandfather's farm to the little creek that meandered through his pasture.

Let that hook get snagged on a root or rock, and into the stream I'd wade to free it. Take no chance on losing that precious bit of bent wire!

Thus, began a lifetime of fishing. I didn't learn to love fishing. I was born loving fishing.

Countless hours have been spent pursuing the sport since those boyhood days. Willow sticks graduated to bamboo poles, then steel casting rods, and finally to the fine fiberglass and graphite equipment we know today.

Two men, my Uncles Ted and Herb, contributed greatly to the fishing pleasures of my youth. Both, I think, realized how deep the yearning within me burned. And on Sunday afternoons, they'd take me along as they fished from leaky rented wooden rowboats. Or in winter, to chisel holes in frozen lakes to set crude tipups, homemade from orange crate slats and wooden spools, for northern pike.

In time came college and a career in forestry, work that allowed me to settle in northern Wisconsin, a land rich with lakes and streams. I fished for the walleyes, muskies, northerns, bass, perch, bluegills and crappies that inhabited those waters. And best of all, the trout streams, each a world of its own, where brooks and browns came to my creel.

Too, I've trolled for barracuda and other saltwater species over the coral reefs of the Bahamas. I've stood in the crashing surf of the North Carolina coast to cast for bluefish and drum. Once, as a serviceman in 1946, I caught rainbow trout from a secluded fish hatchery deep in the mountains of Japan. And days on lakes in the Canadian wilderness where I've caught walleyes in the midst of awe-inspiring beauty and solitude.

Fishing is a lot more than catching fish, however.

There's the laughter of the rapids of a trout stream; the last shafts of the day's sunlight slanting surrealistically upon its face. And there's thunder that echoes through tall white pines; soft veil-like morning mists hanging on the dawn's air; and drowsy dusks that settle as evening comes on, lulling the stream to sleep.

There's the roll of a boat before grey froth-flecked waves pushed before a southwesterly muskie fisherman's breeze; green fronds of lacy underwater vegetation undulating gracefully beneath the surface; swimming muskrats cutting watery wakes back in the bulrushes; and the plaintive notes of yodelling loons floating over lonely, primeval islands.

If one is perhaps so fortunate, there's the sight of a majestic timber wolf padding fearlessly across a frozen, snow-covered remote lake. Maybe a white-headed, white-tailed bald eagle wheeling spectacularly downward to snatch a discarded baitfish from the ice. And ghost-like sun dogs hanging in the gold of a January sunset.

Those are the things that fishing's really made of, I've found.

...The fish are merely a bonus.

Acknowledgements

Some kinds of fishing are best done alone, I've learned. Trout fishing's one. There's no room in a stream for a companion standing thigh-deep nearby, or even within hollerin' distance. Trout fishing is best a solitary experience.

Unless, of course, one counts the company of red-winged blackbirds twittering in the alders or red squirrels scampering across fallen elm trees. Or the vibrant pulse of the water itself pushing against one's boots.

There have been times, however, when I have felt the presence of another on a stream.

On those special mornings, when the world appeared to be particularly beautiful, as I prepared to depart, I'd sometimes tell myself, "Me and God are going to meet down at the crick today...and we're goin' fishin' together!"

I figured God was a trout fisherman too.

And I pondered deeply His creations.

...Then, there are times when fishing is best done in the company of others.

I've fished for sixty years now. There's no way that I can properly credit the multitude of folks with whom I've shared boats, river banks, and frozen lakes. As a boy, two favorite uncles; neighborhood buddies; and later, family members. My wife, Marian; son Mark and Kim, his wife; daughter

Anne and Dave, her husband. And the grandkids; Michelle, Ben, Kyle and Jesse.

Friends by the dozens...those mentioned herein are but a small sample. Mostly men, but some women too. People who brightened days with excited laughter when the fish bit, and outrageous tales when they didn't.

I thank them all. May I have given back as much as I received.

Lastly, a tip of a battered fishing hat to those editors and publishers who saw fit to put into print, over the past eight years, the words that I concocted. Sometimes extraordinary things happen while fishing. On such occasions, I've often remarked to fishing partners, "How does one find the words?"

...I tried.

The Author

Contents

"The author Bob Becker and a Wisconsin Walleye"

The Boat Trade

The boat will come home from winter storage any day now. It's a beauty; sleek and shiny, and it's paint glistens in the sun. The black 18 horse Merc on its transom sparkles for no grease or oil stains yet mar its surface. The whole rig is new, you see.

Oh, I had a good rig before this one, and it had served me well. It was back in 1964 that Bob Link up at Minong had sold it to me. But with 18 years of hours and miles on it, the decision was made to trade.

Last fall found me back at Bob's place checking out the latest in boats, motors and trailers. The usual dickering went on and finally a deal was made...my old rig plus "x" number of dollars to boot. I was satisfied.

Bob's a good man to do business with. "Bring your old outfit up in a couple days and we'll have your new one ready," he told me.

But then, these strange feelings began to set in.

As I worked to strip the old boat down, memories came flooding back, and I started to have second thoughts.

That worn and polished seat up front, for example. People like Bill Waggoner, Earle Gingles and Burt Dahlberg had ridden there. Memories like that are worth a lot. Did you figure those in on the deal, Bob?

And how about that first keeper muskie that son had caught over on Sand Lake out of that boat? Wasn't that father-son handshake across that center seat worth something, Bob?

Then there was that Tony the Tiger sticker out of a breakfast cereal box that was stuck to the side up by the front seat. It said "Don't Pollute Our Lakes." It was a message to everyone sitting up there that I didn't want anything going over the side except anchors and fishing baits. You looked right past that, Bob!

And that yardstick screwed to the top of the center seat! That's where I measured up Momma's muskie out of Big Sis. It came up a quarter-inch shy of the size limit, and I pitched it over the side. She was so mad that she wrote a letter to a downstate paper, and the next Sunday I was chastised in front of the whole state as an unreasonable, inflexible dictator! How much was that worth, Bob?

And Ben, my four-year-old grandson, caught his first bluegills out of that boat while he unmercifully needled his Dad about his fishing ability. Something like that is priceless, Bob!

Oh, I could go on and on. But I know memories, like beauty, are in the eyes of the beholder, and they don't have much market value. So I really don't have any complaints. A deal is a deal!

But there's a couple other things you should know, Bob.

When I brought that old rig up and parked it where you told me to, amongst your array of boats and canoes, you should know that I stopped and took a long, hard look back at it.

And you know what, Bob? I almost changed my mind. And that's the truth.

So 18 years from now when I come back to see you again, please — keep that in mind — because I may be a lot harder to deal with.

A Special Muskie!

The muskie mount came home the other day. Jack Thompson did a good job on it. It's back is arched, and it's toothy mouth is open just as it was a second before it struck my bait that sunny afternoon last September on Sand Lake.

Now, I'm not a trophy fisherman. Over the past 50 years I've caught my share of fish, but this is the first one I've put on the wall. And that may not have happened either had not Momma talked me into it by saying she'd give it to me for Christmas.

It's not a real bragging fish — only 19 pounds and just under 42 inches. But it was a beautifully formed and marked fish. And besides, it was a special fish.

I was fishing with Art "Mr. Muskie" Oehmcke that day. Art spent a lifetime propagating muskies, and it's because of efforts such as his that we know muskie fishing as the quality sport that it is today.

Fall was just coming into its glory that September day. The color was coming on, and the red and gold hues along the shore gave the lake a full-screen technicolor look. A gentle breeze ruffled the water's surface, and a wool shirt felt good.

Sand is one of "my" lakes. I've put a lot of hours on it, and I know it well. How many memories of fish raised here and fish caught there! Art had never fished it; and so it was that we found ourselves drifting over its bars and weedbeds.

Talk went back and forth from old times to new times as we methodically heaved the big baits, retrieved them, always watching for that "follow." Experienced muskie fishermen are realists. They know how many sore arms and backaches go into putting a keeper in the boat. We fished steadily but casually, pausing only to change baits when water conditions warranted a deeper or shallower running lure.

Than, as always, out of nowhere it happened. I was casting a muskie-size Rapala, one of my favorite baits. In the clear water I saw the fish rush the bait and strike.

Instinctively I leaned into the heavy rod to set the hook — perhaps a little too instinctively! Because as the fish passed under the boat, all I could see was 3 1/2 feet of muskie with a foot of Rapala sticking out of its mouth.

"I'll never get 'em, Art!" I said. "He's not hooked good!"

"Take him slow!" came the counsel of Mr. Muskie. He'd been there before.

So with a feather touch on the reel, I played the fish. No pressure, no horsing. Ever so slowly, I nursed the fish up and toward the boat.

Art stood ready with the big, long-handled net; and when the fish swirled on the surface the first time; the net shot out, and the fish came twisting and turning into the boat. I didn't think a 70 year-old duffer could move that fast!

There were the usual "All rights!", the hand shake, and the admirations of what a pretty fish it was. And I remember remarking about the large stomach bulge, wondering what was in it.

That was the action for the day. That night the fish was

hung on the scale at the Super Valu in Spooner and the pictures taken of two tired but smiling fishermen. And that's when Momma told me to have it mounted.

So the call went out to Jack Thompson who has his taxidermy shop out east of Spooner, and a couple days later I brought the frozen fish out to him.

A few days later I stopped in again to pick up the meat from the fish.

"What was in that fish?" I asked.

"You'd never believe this," he said. "That fish had a full-grown female bufflehead duck in its stomach!"

Like I said, it was a special muskie. How often do you catch a fish and a duck on the same cast?

The Nightcrawler is a Survivor

The nightcrawler is a noble beast in my book. I've never known of one having been mounted and put on the wall as a trophy. But I have heard of one that appeared on the Johnny Carson show; and that's getting into some pretty heavy company.

My Uncle Herb introduced me to nightcrawlers back in my early youth.

Oh, I'd dug my share of the common variety of earthworms for fishing bait, and I considered them a dim-witted, slow-thinking critter at best. A few turns of dirt with the shovel always yielded enough to fill an old tin can, more than ample for an afternoon's bullhead fishing in the "crick" that ran through my grandfather's lower pasture.

So when Uncle Herb said we needed some nightcrawlers for a bluegill fishing trip, I figured that chore would be a piece of cake. But when he explained that we'd have to go out after dark to capture them, I began to wonder if he wasn't pulling a naive country boy's leg.

But then Uncle Herb was one of my genuine heroes, right up there with Babe Ruth, Tom Mix, and The Lone Ranger. So I figured I could trust him.

I'd stay overnight at his house, and the next day we'd go fishing.

Just before dark, Unk gave the backyard and garden a good sprinkling. Again my doubts returned. I'd drowned out gophers, but I'd never heard of anyone drowning out worms. Finally, a half hour or so after dark, Uncle Herb announced we were ready, picked up his flashlight and a small pail, and off he went into the backyard with me trailing behind. When he began to shine his light over the grass, I still wasn't sure that I wasn't being had.

But when his hand shot out and the biggest worm I'd ever seen in my life came stretching out of the ground, all my faith in my hero was restored, and then some. This was all right!

My immediate reaction was 'let me get in on some of the action.' Unk looked at me with one of those "OK, if you think you're so smart" looks that you give over-eager kids when you know they're doomed to failure, and proceeded to spot a fat crawler lazily languishing on the grass.

I took one step forward; and zip, Mr. Crawler disappeared from sight. Lesson number one, all worms are not dim-witted.

A second crawler was spotted. This time I tip-toed and slowly reached down to gently pick up the critter. The first touch of my fingers and zip, again it disappeared. Lesson number two, all worms are not slow thinkers.

So from that day on I've had a deep respect for the intelligence level of nightcrawlers.

The crawler is a survivor; peacefully and quietly co-existing with man; aerating and fertilizing the soil; and providing countless little tunnels for rainwater to seep into the soil. The number that are gathered each year by fishermen eager to catch trout, walleyes and bluegills would undoubtedly stagger the mind.

The greatest compliment of all, however, has come in recent years from the fishing bait manufacturers. Imitations made of rubber and plastic cover several pages in all the better fishing equipment catalogs. Now we can even get these phonies perfumed with exotic scents such as strawberry and licorice.

But you can bet there will never be a legitimate substitute for a real, true-to-life, slimey, wiggling nightcrawler. He's got class, and he's a survivor.

I know of no government agency that has taken on the responsibility for looking after the welfare of our nightcrawler population, and I hope it stays that way.

I'd hate the thought of my little nocturnal friends being poked, probed, banded and radio-tagged.

Acourtin' The Beautiful Lady!

I went to see that beautiful lady the other day. We've been romancing together now for about twenty years, I'd say. And the nicest part of the whole affair is that my wife knows all about it.

Not only does Momma know all about it, but there are times when she actually encourages my little adventures. The lady you see is a trout stream.

I hadn't seen her since last fall, and I was eager to pay my respects. I came over the ridge, and there she was; dressed in a new spring outfit of pale green touched off with a necklace of yellow marsh marigolds. With the sunshine reflecting off her face, she was a sight to behold.

Like I said, I've known her quite awhile; and though she's all of 10,000 years old, she's as slim and trim and vibrant as ever.

And then she's got a personality that matches her beauty. The sound of the laughter of her rapids is almost enough to charm me right out of my waders.

Sure, there's a time or two when she puts on a little weight after a two or three inch rain. But a week's diet of dry weather puts her right back into perfect shape.

She has her mood swings, of course. But I've come to know and understand them fairly well. There are days when she's warm and friendly, and the brook and brown trout come easy.

And then there are days when she's cold and unyielding, and I leave her with little more than another memory in my creel.

But the brooks and browns are only a small part of the brood that she rears every year.

There's the little doe for example, that came crashing out of the alders and splashed into her waters not ten feet from me. And the red fox that came trotting down her bank as I stood motionless in one of her pools.

There's the mink that slithers with fluid motion through the tree roots on the water's edge, and the red squirrel that high-tails it across the fallen dead elm.

Then there are the hen mallards, wood ducks and mergansers that feign broken wings as I come sneaking around a bend, doing their best to decoy me away, while their fluffy offspring skitter into the overhanging marsh grass.

And I've had her muskrats with their mouths filled with supper swim almost between my legs. The bittern and blue heron flush with frantic wing beats as I spook them from their frog fishing.

Yes, she's a good parent.

But, as in the best of families, she too has her black sheep. Her rebellious beaver kin do their best to disrupt the order that she tries so hard to maintain.

When things get out of hand, she needs some help; and the wildlife men have to come in with their traps to do their guidance counselling.

And then there are those who don't treat her with the respect she deserves. I find the beer and bait cans on her bottom.

But through it all she bears up very well, and I've come to appreciate the life she lives.

I've been with her you see, when the thunder and lightning crash and echo through her white pines. I've been with her when the dawn is breaking; and she stretches and yawns, and rubs the morning mist from her eyes as the first redwing blackbird twitters back in the willows.

And I've listened to her voice fade into the night as my boots feel for the path out of the valley through which she flows.

What's her name?

Well, now you should know better than to even ask. Old trout fishermen have never been known to kiss and tell.

"A Special Brown Trout"

Carolina Surf Fishing

North Carolina — a land of sunshine, friendly people, tall pine trees, 72 cents a gallon gas and surf fishing. Momma and I are down here on our annual pilgramage to shake hands with Spring, hug the grandchildren and catch some bluefish hopefully.

We're on the New River Air Station, a neat, clean and orderly little city run by the United States Marine Corps just outside Jacksonville. Our son-in-law, Dave Andrea, a career Marine, helps keep the Corps' helicopters flying here. He's also a pretty good guide when it comes to catching bluefish, drum and flounder from the white sand beaches that rim the Atlantic Ocean just a couple of miles to the east.

So on those days that he can get away; we leave Momma, daughter and the grandkids laughing it up; load the car with fishing gear; sneak quietly down the driveway; and head for the beaches. A stop at a fresh fish market for some cut mullet for bait whets my fishing appetite. The showcases are full of all sizes and kinds of salt-water fish.

The highway leaves the city life behind and becomes a corridor through dense stands of eighty-foot loblolly pine trees. Stands that make old foresters drool! Like northern Wisconsin, this is timber country. Truckloads of sawlogs, poles and pulpwood are common on the roads.

We pass a fire lookout tower; and like our North, this is also forest fire country. This spring is already in the "extreme" class, and the papers carry stories every day about the situation.

Ahead lies the low line of sanddunes that marks the beginning of the beach; and as we approach, a tanned bikini-clad young lady stands silhouetted against the blue sky and ocean. What a picture for a Chamber of Commerce brochure!

As we unload our gear, the boom of the surf is music to my ears. What is there about the sound of moving water that soothes the soul? Some say it goes back to our pre-natal days.

The smell of the salty ocean air hits me, and my lungs think I've died and gone to heaven. But then, they should really know better.

Surf fishing – a simple but different style of fishing.

Heavy action, nine-foot rods are typical. Reels are of the open-faced, large capacity variety loaded with as much thirty pound monofilament as you can get on. A four-ounce sinker is clipped to the end of the line, and two stout steel-leadered drop hooks are attached above the sinker a foot or two. Strips of cut mullet are the bait.

The cast is made as far out into the breakers as one can heave the heavy sinker, and the slack line is reeled in. The technique is to keep a tight line so that the hit from the bottom feeding fish can be felt.

We're after bluefish primarily. They travel in schools; and when a pack moves in, the action is fast and furious. In past years, they've averaged three to five pounds.

But we're here at the early end of the season, and the fish aren't cooperating. I place the rod butt into a rod holder, and

I settle back into a lawn chair which I've brought along for just such an emergency.

If you can't catch fish, you can always enjoy the fishing. White gulls and terns wheel in the cloudless sky overhead; and a wedge of goose-size birds, probably migrating brant, wing their way northward up the coast. A squadron of pouch-billed pelicans slips by riding the wind barely three feet above the water.

The sunshine, the salt air, the sound of the surf, the sandwiches; they're getting to me. The eyelids are getting heavy.

What the heck! There's always tomorrow.

That Would Be Serious!

The project out at the Tree Farm would have to wait. My first morning look out the back window told me that it was no day to be running a power saw. A steady rain was falling from clouds that hung so low they seemed to be touching the top of the big elm tree in the back yard.

But that wasn't too serious. There's an old saying in the woods, "If it's raining too hard to work, go fishing."

My first thought was to try the walleyes. But when a clap of thunder shook the morning air, I ruled that out. I don't like to be in a boat when lightning is flashing.

But that wasn't too serious. There were a couple of trout streams down in Barron County that Jerry Perkins, one of the fisheries medics down there, had been bragging up. I'd give them a try.

So with Jerry's handy dandy map on the dash board, I packed up my gear and headed the pickup south on Highway 63.

My first stop was at a bridge where a stream noted for brook trout crossed a town road. I looked at the sky as I slipped on the waders. Naw, I wouldn't need a rain jacket and headed downstream through the alders and marsh grass. I eyeballed the stream as I hiked in a half mile or so and was surprised to see the water so low.

But that wasn't too serious. I'd fished low water lots of times.

So I slipped into the stream and began to fish my way back to the bridge. Three nice brook trout quickly came to the creel.

And that's when the thunder boomed again. I quickened the pace, but the shower caught me. By the time I reached the truck, the top half of me was soaked real good.

But that wasn't too serious. I've been wet many times.

After a cup of coffee and a sandwich, I decided to give a second stream a look. A short drive and I found myself pulling on the waders once more. This time the rain jacket would go on too.

It wasn't my day for weather. Half way into the stream, the sun came out; and I felt like a walking microwave oven with the switch turned on.

But that wasn't too serious. Maybe I'd lose a couple pounds.

Now to get down to the stream I had to pick my way down a steep bank. I don't mean just steep. I mean steep steep. I was inching my way down the rain-slicked clay when my feet went out from under me. If it hadn't been for a convenient sapling, I would have wrapped myself around a popple tree.

But that wasn't too serious. I slipped down a red clay bank into the Brule River once.

I hit the stream, and it didn't take long to see that the fish were in a hitting mood. I don't think I fished 200 yards, when five nice browns and two very respectable brooks joined the three brookies in the creel.

It was some of the best trout fishing I've had in a long time. Perkins was right. I paused for a couple minutes, loaded and lit my pipe, and began my wade back downstream. My head was up enjoying the wonders of nature; the trilliums along the bank, the sounds of the spring bird life.

I didn't see that confounded sunken log lying on the bottom. When my boot touched it, I knew I was in trouble. Between my forward momentum and the current pushing me from behind, over I went. Now I'll tell you, about three buckets of cold trout stream water down the front of your waders will give you a thrill.

But that wasn't too serious. I've gone over the top of my waders quite a few times.

As I fell forward, I made a desperate grab for my pipe and I hung on to it for dear life as my hand hit the bottom. I could have easily lost it you see.

And that would have been serious.

Small Businessmen

I like to do business with small businessmen. The smaller, the better.

Every summer, especially if we're having a dry year, my night crawler supply runs out. And I'm in big trouble with my trout fishing.

I try to avoid the problem. About mid-May each year I lay in a good batch of crawlers in two old wash tubs down in the basement. But my cache is usually depleted about August. And it's then that I start looking for those little hand-lettered signs along the highways that read "NIGHT CRAWLERS FOR SALE".

Now, over the years I've bought night crawlers from grandmothers, housewives and old retired gents. But my favorite crawler businesses are those that are run by kids.

Usually there are two brothers in business. The older will be about eleven, the younger about nine. The oldest, he's the president of the firm; and the youngest, he's the vice president. They don't wear fancy three-piece suits or flashy sales uniforms, just faded bluejeans and tattered tennis shoes.

Most of the time there's a sister hanging around; and though she wants desperately to be, she's not an employee or even a stockholder in the firm.

Then there's always a nondescript dog, one with an original name like Brownie. He's the plant guard, and he runs a close security check on everyone that enters.

I pull in the driveway, and the President and the Vice President are there in a hurry to greet me. They believe in good customer relations.

"Hello," I say; "I see you've got night crawlers for sale."

"That's right, mister," the President says.

"Yup," says the Vice President.

By now Brownie is eyeing me with one of those 'make one false move buster, and I'll nail ya' looks. I keep positioning myself so that my back is never turned on Brownie.

"How much are your worms?" I ask.

"Sixty cents a dozen," the President answers. "Yup," nods the Vice President.

"Good," I say; "I'll take five dozen."

Eyes light up at the prospect of a big sale.

"They're back in the barn," says the President. "Yup," echoes the Vice President.

By now sister has shyly slipped into the circle, and together we walk out to the barn. I keep a close eye on Brownie.

Inside, the two businessmen rummage through their inventory of assorted tin cans and come up with a good-sized coffee can, their five-dozen-special container. As the two officers begin to sift through an old dirt-filled wash boiler, I ask a dumb question.

"How do you get these worms?"

"We get 'em at night," says the President. "Yup, after it rains," says the Vice President, beginning to show some of the power of his office.

"There's one!" exclaims sister.

The two officers slowly turn and give her a silent stare that would freeze a jug of Prestone. Their message sent, they again return to counting worms.

"There's your five dozen mister," says the President.

"Good, how much do I owe you?" I ask.

Well, now there's some fast modern math practiced on four hands. "That'll be three dollars," I'm told.

I hand over the three bucks and top it off with a couple quarters.

"Gee, thanks mister," beams the President. "Yeah, thanks a lot," seconds the Vice President. Brownie wags his tail for the first time. Sister is still thawing out.

I say my good-bye and head the pickup down the driveway escorted by Brownie. And as I look back in the rearview mirror, all I can see is bluejeaned rearends and tennis shoes as the two businessmen head for the bank with their loot.

I come to a stop for the highway and Brownie wags his tail again, this time in earnest. I'm OK. I've passed inspection. I can come back.

And I chuckle as I head down the road. It's a pleasure to do business with small businessmen.

We Came Close!

There we were. The combined ages of the two of us added up to 132 years. Yet there we were, double-layered with raingear, bouncing around in a boat. The downpour from the lead-colored sky sounded like birdshot as it ricocheted off the hood of my parka. The stiff wind kicked up white-capped waves, and streaks of frothy foam laced the water's surface.

Yet there we were; telling each other what a great day it was to fish, that we'd put a good muskie in the boat before quitting time. Common sense said we'd be wiser sitting in a warm, dry living room in front of a checkerboard.

But that could never be. Let the muskie-fishing germ infect your bloodstream; and there's no cure, no hope. It's a terminal situation; no vaccine, no medication can touch it. You learn to live with it.

Art Oehmcke and I were out there to do a re-run. A year ago on the same lake we'd performed our act of magic and pulled a trophy muskie out of the hat. And there we were, going back to the well again.

And we came close.

Six hours we spent heaving the big baits. Plugs that weigh a pound or better; flashy spoons with white pork rind strips that danced from over-sized hooks; bushy-haired bucktails that fluttered with tantalizing action as they skimmed submerged weed beds.

Art is a world-class optimist. We match up real well in a boat. There's as much enthusiasm, as much hope, as much confidence on the last cast of the day as there is on the first. The muskie, the fish of a thousand casts; or is it 10,000? You have to be a "can do" thinker. If you're not, you won't last an hour in the muskie fishing game.

"Come on; you green-eyed, lantern-jawed pups! I know you're out there!" I heard it a dozen times from the front seat.

And there was "Ludwig," the foot-long sucker that trailed the boat, dangling from a cork bobber bigger than a baseball. "Go get 'em, Ludwig! Get to work out there!" A dozen times I heard it.

And we came close.

On the second drift a small "legal" came up, following my Rapala right to the side of the boat. I figure-eighted the plug while the fish trailed it nose-tight to the lure; its bronze body shimmering below the surface; until it tired of the game.

And I listened to Art's tales of the old days, days well before my time. Long ago Conservation Department directors like Harley MacKenzie, Ed Vanderwall and Ernie Swift. Of governors going back to the Julius Heil administration of the 1930's. Of how it was to be a young fisheries biologist back in those days.

Stories of the famous he'd guided over the years. How Gypsy Rose Lee had come to northern Wisconsin to catch a muskie, and how indeed she did. How Edward R. Murrow had shared a boat with him. Stories that joined others he'd told me on past trips; Ted Williams, Prince Harald of Norway, Warren Knowles.

How he'd fished with Mel Ellis, an outdoor writer and author, whom I knew only through weekly columns and books on my bookshelf. How they broke ice one cold November morning to fish and caught a twenty-five pounder a long time ago.

And we came close ourselves.

The fish came up over a weedy bar. "There's one, Art! A good keeper!" I exclaimed. But just as quickly, the fish was gone under the boat, just another memory.

But they don't call Art Oehmcke "Mister Muskie" for nothing. He'd been there before, lots of times. I didn't even notice as he turned and shot the big jerk bait back off the other side of the boat into the wind.

But I did pay attention when I heard his grunt, and I turned to see the swirl in the rolling waves. Twice he leaned into the rod to set the hook. The muskie shot to the surface splashing in the foam; its emerald-green back shining; its white belly flashing in the greyness; its mighty head shaking to spit the fraud that had betrayed it. And then it was gone.

We'd come close. A quarter of an inch might have made the difference. And that's close, mighty close!

The Young Guy

I took this young guy out ice fishing the other day. Over the years I've taken a lot of young guys out fishing; people all the way from four-year-old toddlers on up to that point in time where "young" changes to "old."

Now, I like to take young folks out fishing. I like to watch them having fun catching a fish or two; like to see them enjoying the outdoors; like to try to answer their questions.

So when the phone rang and this young guy was on the other end asking if I was interested in going ice fishing, what else could I say but "Sure." And when the appointed hour to meet came about, he was on time; a good start, a good indication that he was serious about the whole thing.

As we headed out to the lake, we rapped about the ins-and-outs of ice fishing. And yes, I pumped him up a little bit with a couple glowing tales of past trips back in my youth, back when I was young.

By the time we hit the boat landing, he had a good head of steam up. It didn't take him long to gather up his gear and stow it in my sled. And as we headed across the frozen surface of the lake, he even grabbed the rope and helped me pull the load. Now that's a smart thing for any young guy to do, a good way to make some brownie points.

The day was perfect; sunny and quiet, ideal for fishing in

comfort. We'd be after northern pike, a fish that neither asks for nor gives any respect; a fish with an uncomplicated country-boy personality. A fish that says, "Hang a bait out there, buster; and I'll take you on!"

Well, the young guy and I walked down the lake a quarter mile or so, and we came to a place where some other fishermen had been the day before. The young guy was eager to get his lines in the water. And I remembered how I'd had the same feeling many, many times.

So when we came to an old open hole in the ice, the young guy said, "I'll put a tip-up in here. This looks OK to me."

Well, now the hole didn't look OK to me. Barely six inches across, you'd have a tough time pulling a respectable northern through it. But then, young people have to learn, I thought. And besides, how much advice should a person give?

Now, the young guy had brought a pail of minnows along, but I planned to use dead smelt for bait. I guess maybe I'd pumped him up too much on the ride out about how good smelt were for catching northerns.

Because the young guy turned to me and asked if he could "borrow" one of my smelt. "Sure," I said. But I couldn't quite figure out how a bait that had been chomped on by a big northern was going to be in any kind of shape to be returned. But then, he was young. Young folks say things like that.

Well, the six tip-ups were finally all in; and as luck would have it, up goes the young guy's flag, the tip-up with the borrowed smelt. I watched as he ran and skidded across the hundred yards of slippery ice, eager to land the first fish. I watched as he lifted the line and set the hook. And I watched as he struggled to get the fish through the tiny hole; finally reaching into the water with his hand to lift the six pound fish out on the ice.

As he came dragging the fish over to me, I chuckled as he said, his face glowing, "This is fun! Can I borrow another smelt?"

"Sure," I said.

Fifteen minutes go by and bang, up goes that smelt flag again. Once more the young guy slips and slides across the ice. Once more he sets the hook, and once more the battle is on. Out of the hole comes another six pounder, a twin to the first.

By now the smile on his face was reaching the ear flaps on his cap. It was good to see this young guy so happy.

The afternoon sped by; and as the sun slipped beneath the tree line, the young guy caught his fifth northern, his limit.

His face beamed as he looked at me and said, "My wife isn't going to believe this when I bring these fish in the house." I felt good for him.

We stopped at his pickup, and I helped him load his gear in the darkness. And he looked at me and said, "This was the best day of ice fishing I've ever had in my life!"

Not a bad compliment; especially when it comes from a young guy that's only seventy-two years young.

Another Time...Another Place

They pulled up alongside of me as I sat parked on the little boat landing watching my tipups. There were four of them; the father, mother and two young boys; brothers probably eight and ten years old. A family fishing trip.

I smiled as they got out and the two boys, dressed in their snowmobile suits, immediately began their horseplay; pushing, shoving, knocking each other down in the snow. It would be a good day.

I watched as the father opened the topper of the pickup and unloaded the gear, a green plastic pail full of tipups, red flags sticking up; a blue ice auger, a styrofoam minnow pail. And they headed out onto the frozen lake, the father leading the way, the boys dancing around, the young mother following; proud, enjoying her family.

I watched as the father drilled the holes and set the lines. I couldn't hear the words, but I could easily read the sign language. I got the message as he gathered his two sons around him, as he measured the water's depth, as he explained how the bait minnows should be hooked, how the flag on the tipup would be released when a fish hit the bait.

When the lines were all in, they returned to their truck, the father and the mother sitting in the cab listening to the radio. I could faintly hear the muffled talk going on between them, the communication.

The two boys pulled a red plastic sled from the back of the pickup and began their belly-flopping down the incline to the lake. Friendly belly-flopping for about two turns apiece. Then it was back to the horseplay, the dumping of each other into the snow amidst shrill shouts and loosely-packed snowballs.

The father stepped out of the pickup. A flag was up! And he gathered the two boys in tow and headed out to the tipup. I watched as he positioned the oldest boy next to the hole, as he explained how the line should be handled, as he jerked his arm to show how the hook should be set.

Slowly the boy lifted the tipup from the ice and grasped the line. A few seconds pause and the boy's arm shot up over his head, the tipup flying through the air a dozen feet. I watched as the boy struggled to land the fish, his child inexperience showing. And finally, the father reached down; and with a smooth swing of his arm skidded the northern pike onto the ice, the two boys jumping and clapping their hands.

I watched as they dragged the fish back to the landing, and I couldn't resist getting out as they passed by. "That's a nice fish," I said to the boy. "You did a good job of landing it."

"Thanks," the boy replied. "Dad helped me."

"Not much!" the father shot back.

"How big is it?" I asked.

"I'd say about twenty-eight inches," the father offered.

"Oh, I think it'll go more than that," and I pulled the tape measure from my coat and laid it along the fish, thirty inches on the nose. The smile on the boy's face was about to sprain his cheek muscles.

There'll be another time, another place. It's down the road

of life a good ways yet. But it'll come. Maybe it'll be in a kitchen over a cup of coffee.

The boy will have become a man. His hands will be big, large enough to circle the coffee cup; and his shoulders will be broad, heavy-muscled. The father's face will be lined, and he'll move a little slower. There'll be blue-grey wood smoke in the hair at his temples.

They'll talk. They'll face each other, look deep into each other's eyes, and they'll talk. Talk about what's going right, about what's not going so right; talk about the heavier things in life.

And there'll be a pause, a break in their conversation, as their thoughts slip back in time.

"Dad, do you remember that time you took us ice fishing?" the boy-man will slowly say, barely above a whisper. "The time I caught that big northern?"

"I sure do," the father will answer.

"That was sure fun," the boy-man will add. "We should go fishing one of these days."

"Let's do that," the father will say.

There'll be another pause, another silence as thoughts once more drift back through the years. The boy-man will slowly raise his coffee cup to his lips. The father will stare into his cup, then softly clear his throat.

And then they'll go back to talking about the heavier things in life.

Ice Shacks

This friend of mine was talking to me the other day about ice fishing. And he proceeded to tell me that he was building an ice fishing shack. Now I know a little bit about ice fishing shacks, having owned a couple of those hummers. Having one is sort of like having teen-agers in the family; some headaches, 'er responsibilities I mean.

Take the shack I had down on Shawano Lake for instance. Now Shawano is a big lake, some 6,000 acres in size and about seven miles long. Each year there's a couple thousand shacks on it. And I just had to have one too. I just knew I'd catch more fish and have a lot more fun if I did.

So I looked around and sure enough, I stumbled onto this little beauty that the owner was willing to let me take off his hands for the outrageous price of $15.00. Well-built with steel pipe for the frame, a good northwest blizzard could have rolled it the length of the lake without hurting it. The price even included a steel folding chair.

Well, I couldn't resist a good deal like that and I forked over the fifteen bucks. I was so pleased with my find that I even painted a little sign that read "Ice is Nice" and nailed it over the door. Little did I realize that my responsibilities, 'er headaches, were about to begin.

For starters there was the sweet-talking that I had to do to get my new-found toy hauled out on the lake. Then there was the snow and slush that I had to buck with the car to get to it. I soon found out too that you don't leave your valuable tip-ups and ice auger in your shack. Things like that have a tendency to disappear in the dark of night.

But my ultimate responsibility, 'er headache, came one sloppy night when I awoke about midnight to the drum of raindrops against the bedroom window. Like a beacon, that shack flashed before my eyes. I could just see that hummer slowly settling into the slush of the lake. And I just knew by morning that the weather would turn cold, and there my little palace would be, frozen in six inches of ice.

What to do? The more I thought about it, the more it became crystal clear that I really didn't have any choice. Get up, get dressed and go prop that stupid shack up.

Well, Momma murmured something about fruitcake ice fishermen, but away I went.

Now I'll be the first to admit that I've pulled my share of less-than-intelligent stunts. But driving out on Shawano Lake at one o'clock in the morning in a driving rainstorm is near the top of the list.

There I was, prying up the corners of that now less-than-beautiful shack with a crowbar and stuffing chunks of two-by-fours under the corners. If someone with a big net and a white coat had been waiting as I drove off the lake, I wouldn't have been at all surprised.

So that little experience came back to me the other day as my friend talked glowingly about the shack he was building.

"Good," I said to him, "Now you can have all the fun of chopping it out of the ice come March 15."

"No problem!" he says. "All I'm going to do is take my 30.06 out there, put on some ear muffs, shut the door, and let a round go inside. The concussion will break all that ice loose."

Now this was a new approach, and I've been pondering it ever since my friend explained it to me.

Well, let me say right here that I have some very serious reservations about this innovative idea. You see, I have this very real concern that if a 30.06 concussion will break an ice shack loose; then there is also the strong possibility that it will also break loose a couple of eardrums, ear muffs or no ear muffs; not to mention any and all assorted wax deposits therein.

So please, please don't try this new scheme. An idea like this has to be very thoroughly researched. Let my friend do the research. Let him do the pilot study.

I'll be seeing him again along toward spring. And I'll check with him on how his brilliant plan works.

I expect I'll walk up to him and ask, "How did that idea of yours to free your ice fishing shack with your 30.06 work?"

He may just cup his hand to his ear and say, "Eh? What's that you say?"

If he does, I won't even bother to repeat the question.

Bozo

I call him Bozo; he's a dog.

The night was still pitch black as I parked the pickup alongside my favorite crappie lake one recent winter morning. I was plenty early, and I flipped on the dome light to look at my watch. Six o'clock it said. I wouldn't have to hurry.

I unloaded my gear; the sled, power auger, three rods, the minnow pail, my insulated pants and jacket; and eased my way down the slope to the ice. A thin sliver of silver was just beginning to show above the tree line across the lake to the east.

As I began my walk following the faint trail on the ice, I spotted the small dark dot silhouetted against the white snow a couple hundred yards to the north. For a second, I wasn't sure what it was, and I stopped. But then I realized it was my fishing partner, and I gave a low whistle.

Like a spring released from tension he leaped forward, recognizing me; and in seconds he was dancing about my feet, glad to see me, the first human of the morning. As I continued the walk out to where we fish crappies together, he cut big circles on the dead run around me, leading me.

We've fished together two winters now. He's a character, one of those uncomplicated country dogs that patrols his territory without flash or fuss. There's nothing pretentious about him. What you see is what you get. Just a brown and black pooch with two floppy ears that refuse to stand up straight. I doubt that he has those so-called "papers" that bloodline dogs point to when they go to prove their ancestry. But he's got two enduring qualities going for him. One, he's friendly; and two, he's intelligent.

Take last year for example, when he first started keeping me company. He didn't understand the fine art of fishing crappies. And there were times when I didn't appreciate at all his getting tangled up in my monofilament lines. It's not easy to unravel twenty-five feet of line from a dog that's bent on playing a game of "catch me if you can."

And anyone that has ever fished with me will vouch to the fact that I can get very serious about little things like that, especially if the fish are biting.

But he's learned and learned well. Now all I have to do is reach for a rod, and he jumps out of the way.

When the rod is again laid down on the ice and the blaze orange bobbers are quietly standing at attention waiting for a bite, then he'll return to my feet to playfully tug at my mittens or nuzzle my arms for some petting.

But it isn't all fun and games. Let a car come around the curve on the town road, and his ears and eyes perk up. Someone's invading his domain. Who is it? And let a snowmobile or a tractor start, and away he goes to check it out.

Then there are his trips across the lake, always the same route. Over to the point, through the marsh grass and into the swamp timber. Why? Maybe he's got a dog friend over there that he has to pay a social call to every now and then.

The other day he appeared just as I started to drill my fishing holes. This time he had a dried-up, oversized hamburger bun in his mouth that he carried the quarter mile from where he lives. He sat down next to the sled and laid the bun in the snow. "Let's have lunch together," he seemed to be saying, and he proceeded to noisily grind the bun into bits. When it was gone, he washed it down with a long drink of cold lake water lapped up from one of my crappie holes. How's that for a country character?

He's a buddy of mine and I truly hope he makes it through another year of dodging dog dangers. I want him around next winter you see, to keep me company when the fish don't bite and the days get long, lonely.

And until someone tells me otherwise, I'll just keep on calling him Bozo.

Old Dumpy!

Old Dumpy, I call her. That's not her real name; that's just what I call her. She's one of my trout stream friends.

As trout streams go, she's no beauty. When good looks were handed out for trout streams, she must have been dozing under the bedrock. In fact, she's downright unattractive. But that's the thing I like best about her. Other fishermen you see, leave her alone.

There are no rippling rapids that send their laughter across the countryside, telling the world, "I'm a beautiful trout stream. Come visit me!" She's just a slow-moving little thing that meanders and plods her way through the marshes and alder swamps.

And there's another thing that I like about her. You won't find boot-trodden paths along her banks. You won't find them because there's mud and mire and brush so thick that it claws at your cap and fishing vest.

You won't find the forked sticks of the bank fishermen poking up. And you won't find the beer cans on her bottom, the cardboard worm boxes left behind. Cans and boxes that are light enough to be carried in but too heavy to be carried out.

Oh, I see a sign or two of another fisherman that comes to court her. There are the broken branches on the alders where someone has opened up a little alley to make a cast. But the branch stubs are old; and maybe, I hope, the fisherman had no luck; maybe he won't return.

And she's got something else going for her. She doesn't raise a lot of trout. Fish a mile of her and you might get a dozen or two bites. She's no better probably than a Class Two stream on the DNR fish manager's rating scale.

Add up all of her good points, and she'd never get past the preliminary judging in a trout stream beauty contest. She's just one of those plain-Jane streams; without much personality or talent; flat, shallow, pudgy, a little on the dumpy side. And that's how she got her name.

But I go to see her, especially early in the trout season when the other more beautiful, vivacious lady streams are getting a lot of attention. It's then that I appreciate Old Dumpy's charm, her true beauty. I can wade a mile up through her swamps, and I can lose the whole world.

I paid her a visit the other day. And a beautiful day it was! The sun wasn't out. The sky was a gorgeous grey; there wasn't a speck of blue in sight. A northeast wind was swirling in off Lake Superior bringing in a fine cool temperature. The wool shirt under my rain jacket felt good.

I stepped into her cold waters, welcomed the gentle nudge of her current. I'd wade that mile, and I'd enjoy every minute of it. If I didn't get a bite; if I didn't catch a fish, the day would still be a good one.

Maybe she was glad to see me too because we had fun together. I hadn't gone a hundred yards when a pair of drake mallards swooshed over my head, over the alders, so close that I could feel the rush of air from their wing beats. And they plopped down ahead of me, their white tail feathers fanned to put on the brakes.

Another hundred yards and the first trout came to the creel, a chunky twelve-inch brown, from a snag-filled pool at the foot of a narrow little run. Then another brown from the run itself.

Slowly I worked my way up that mile, fishing old memories. Fishing bank cuts and runs where I'd taken fish in years past. Enjoying the yellow marsh marigolds, the blue violets peeking out along the banks. Picking up a brown here, a brookie there.

And then her goodbye kiss. A sluggish bend where the green marsh grass is already curving into her waters. I felt the fish pick up the crawler, felt it run back under the grassy bank. I felt the tick-tick as it worked the bait, and I set the hook. The light rod bowed as the fish fought in the tangle. Finally I moved the trout out into the stream, and in a minute or two I lifted it from the water. Sixteen inches the ruler said, a solid two pounds.

Dumpy, you're a sweetheart!

"Joe Weiss and a trophy Musky"

Muskiosis Maxima

Well, it's midsummer again, the time when that terrible fishing disease strikes. "Muskiosis maxima", I call it. But, more commonly, it's known as the "big muskie" disease. And there's a lot of it going around these days.

It's a terrible malady, striking otherwise perfectly rational men, and maybe a woman or two, though I've never personally witnessed such a case. Eyes glaze, stare off into space, hands tremor, and arms convulsively jerk head-high; as if setting a hook into the gaping jaws of a giant, green-eyed monster swimming in the victim's imagination.

I know! I've been there! I've had the malady! In fact, I've still got it. For it's incurable,and only in remission, just waiting for a chance to lay me low once more.

Like the other day when its recurring pangs of pain struck.

Our little fishing club had scheduled its first outing of the year, over on one of my favorite muskie lakes. And I was geared for my first try this year at the beasts.

Now, the weather was a bit blustery what with thunderstorms hanging around. I had to take it easy, the boat bouncing across the rough water, as I pulled away from the landing. Yet, dirty weather's usually good for muskie fishing. And I eased my way to the northeast corner of the lake, sheltered somewhat, and began my casting; heaving a bucktail over a submerged weedbed undulating gracefully below the gray water's surface.

And in pulled another boat, one I didn't recognize. But the guy in it I did...Charlie Tollander. Now Charlie's a good muskie fisherman. He works hard at it.

"How you doin'?" he hollers across the hundred yards of water between us. "Just got here," I answer. "How about you?"

"Can't hook 'em today! I've had four hits, but haven't hooked a single one," he comes back. "But have you seen Joe's fish? He's got a good one!"

Now, the Joe he was talking about, I quickly figured, had to be Joe Weiss, another dyed-in-the-wool, rock 'em-sock 'em muskie chaser.

Well, I made a couple passes over my weedbed and decided to hit another further up the lake. The half-mile run went quickly, and as I eased into position, here's another boat. And, as fate would have it, there's Joe Weiss aboard.

A couple hand waves, and I slip alongside. "Hear you caught a nice one," I greet him.

"Yup, a 45-incher!" he says and lifts the lid from the live box built into his boat. From it, comes one of the prettiest muskies I've seen in a long time; a hefty, broad-backed fish that would weigh out close to 25 pounds.

And as Joe and the muskie posed for a picture, that's when I felt the first faint stirrings of the Muskiosis germs within me. Blood pressure rising, adrenaline pumping, realities of life fading! I'll tell you, it wasn't easy fighting off the attack!

It didn't get any better later in the afternoon either...as the gang gathered on a little island for our customary shorelunch. There we were, forty of us, grown men, standing around the fire clad in olive-drab rain suits, all talking about the same thing...muskies!

"You should've seen the one Dean had on!" Bill Barton says. "Came right out of the water and stood on its tail, almost as big as Joe's!"

And two guys, talking about the merits of graphite rods! "Graphite's a lot better than fiberglass," one says. "Yeah," the other agrees. "You can cast all day and never get tired!"

Oh, no, I think! Now, I gotta have a new rod, one made of graphite! Just what I need...another reason to stand all day in a rocking boat, frying my brain in a hot sun, driven to chasing lunker fish that lurk, who knows where, in our lakes.

That's what Muskiosis does to you.

Don't catch it!!

Old Timer

The yellow windbreaker stood out in the green foliage.

I saw him ahead as I worked my way up one of my favorite trout streams. Who was it, I wondered as I slowly waded toward the little log bridge where he sat on a red five-gallon pail. His line dangled in the fast flow of the stream swollen by the two-inch rain of the night before. I could see that he was old.

Quietly I fished to within a hundred feet of him, then got out of the water into the tall marsh grass. "The rest of the stream is yours, Old Timer;" I thought as I picked my way through the muck toward him.

He hadn't seen me yet. Maybe it was my camoflage waders and rain jacket. Then maybe his eyesight and hearing weren't as good as they used to be. He sat hunched over, concentrating on the tip of his fishing pole, waiting for a trout to bite.

I didn't want to startle him. When I figured he could hear me, I gave him the old standard fisherman's greeting.

"How they biting?"

"Just lost one," he came back looking up, a broad smile creasing his face. "Where did you come from?"

"Oh, I waded up from the town road," I answered.

"Can't do that any more. I've got arthritis too bad." And

then I saw the stout cane lying beside him.

"I've got to find places like this where I can fish without walking too much."

And so began our visit. For an hour we talked, swapping trout fishing tales. How as a boy his uncle used to take him fishing and tie him with a harness rope to a tree alongside a good hole. "And I'd catch my limit," he said proudly.

How he's from Minnesota and comes to Wisconsin to hunt and fish trout. How he's got a favorite spot over on the Clam River, a hole so good that he calls it "trout town."

How he was fishing there one dark night and hooked what he thought to be a lunker trout, only to suddenly have it wrap itself around his leg. And with his flashlight in his mouth, he was forced to decapitate with his knife a huge snake.

And I told him one of my own. How a few weeks before I'd found just downstream from him a brown trout dead and caught in the weeds. A fish almost two feet long that would have gone four pounds. And how on examining it, I discovered a tail sticking out of its throat, the tail of a six-inch chub that it had choked on.

He'd said his name was Fred.

"Fred," I asked, "How old are you?"

"I'm eighty-five," he told me. "I worked for thirty-five years for the Minneapolis water department."

"But for ten years from 1941 to 1951 I was a radio announcer for WCCO on the Cedric Adams Show. Introduced Adams for all his shows. Some of the stuff we pulled back in those days we'd get shot for today."

"What's your name?" he asked.

I told him and said I too do a little "show" business, told him about my writing.

"An outdoor writer, eh? Well, I want to write down your

name and phone number. I go down to Arkansas every year wild boar hunting. I want to bring you some bacon from those wild pigs. It's nice and lean."

And then another tale.

"I've got to tell you about the time I was fishing here once. I had a little red float on to help me see my line. My eyes aren't the best, you see. Well, a kingfisher flew out of that tree over there and grabbed that red float and flew off with it. But then out of nowhere this big hawk dives down and nails the kingfisher. So there I am with a kingfisher and a hawk on my line! And that's the gospel truth."

"Fred," I said, "How would you like a couple trout?" And I unbuckled the creel and laid two nice browns out on the old bridge.

His eyes brightened, and he stuck out a gnarled mitt for a handshake.

"That's great! My doctors tell me that I shouldn't go trout fishing any more. They say they'll find me face down in the mud." And he paused.

"But I tell them; if you ever do, don't feel sorry for me."

Fred, you can bet every time I come up to that little bridge back in the woods...you're going to be there.

Thanks, Son!

We don't get to fish together very often any more. Maybe we get out a couple times a year. There was a time when we went a couple times a week. "This is like old times," I said as I cut the motor on the boat. He'd already rummaged through the tackle box and laid out an array of muskie plugs and bucktails on the center seat. "That it is, Dad! That it is!" he responded.

———————

He was probably four years old. We were crappie fishing from the bank of the Somo River near Tomahawk. I'd bought him a lightweight bamboo pole that he could handle; rigged it with light line, a panfish hook and a little plastic bobber.

"I want my bobber by that stump," he told me as I hooked on a small minnow, his eyes bright with excitement.

I flipped the line alongside the stump and handed him the pole. The ripples had barely quieted on the water when "plunk" the bobber disappeared. "Pull," I told him.

He lifted the pole, and the fish almost jerked it from his small hands. This would be no ordinary fish, and I reached over to give him a hand. The line cut circles in the water, the cane pole creaked from the strain; and finally together we slid a seven pound walleye up on the sand.

———————

The day was better suited for an artist, someone to paint the scarlets, crimsons and golds of the maples and oaks that bathed in the Indian Summer sunshine on the shores of Sand Lake.

— — — — — —

He was probably nine. The family was vacationing at Louie Johnson's resort back in the woods on Mason Lake over in Price County. He was getting pretty good with a rod and reel, the bird-nest backlashes becoming less-and-less frequent.

The spinner dropped next to a tree top lying in the water, and a fish was on. His first muskie, under-size, but nevertheless his first.

— — — — — —

I put the boat on a drift that would take us over the weedy bar. I wanted him to fish it.

"Isn't this where I caught my first legal muskie?" he asked me.

— — — — — —

He was fourteen. A Sunday afternoon trip. We'd pounded that same Sand Lake with no luck. Then as the sun touched the tree line, a drift over that same weedbed. He could handle a rod with the best now, the bucktail lining through the air with smooth rhythm.

"I got one, Dad!" he hollered from the front of the boat. The fish sounded deep, a couple runs, and I gaffed it for him. Thirty-four inches, his first legal muskie.

— — — — — —

We talked, cussed the fish mildly for not cooperating. "Let's take a break," I said; and we pulled in for a sit in the shade.

"Remember the time I got hooked by that muskie?" I asked.

"I'll never forget that day," he came back.

_____

He was seventeen. We were fishing Lake Winter, a new flowage. Recently flooded, dotted with dead trees and brush, it was putting out a couple hundred muskies a summer. And we just had to try it.

The red-and-white injured minnow plug skipped along between the tree stubs. A mighty splash, and a muskie nailed it. Barely legal, I quickly landed it—fully intending to release it.

Gently holding it, I worked the pliers to remove the hooks from its jaw. Then a sudden slippery twist, and a treble hook sunk deep into my forefinger. Now I had a writhing muskie in one hand, and a plug embedded in the other.

"Mark Becker, Age 5"

He reached over, took the pliers, and with all the strength he could muster, cut the shank of the hook setting me free.

_____

We fished the day out, loaded the boat, said our goodbyes, and headed for our homes.

_____

He's a grown man now. And he's got sons of his own. He's busy flying around the country, occupied with production problems and profit-and-loss statements. We don't get to go fishing together too much any more.

_____

Thanks for going along, Son. We didn't catch any keepers this time...but I sure caught more than my limit of good memories.

Fish Shocking

"Wear your longjohns; it's going to be cold! Meet us at the Ranger Station at six o'clock."

Those were Stan Johannes' instructions over the phone. Stan is DNR's fish biologist for Burnett and Washburn Counties.

We'd be going fishing, something that doesn't take much arm twisting to get me to do.

But this would be a different kind of fishing. Our rods would be twenty-foot fiberglass poles. The lure would be an electrical charge from a generator. And the line would be six-foot electrodes dragging through the water.

Electro-fishing, it's called. More commonly it's referred to as fish shocking. The ultimate in fishing techniques, it's guaranteed to catch fish even when they're not biting, when everything else fails.

More properly, it's a method used to sample a fish population in lakes and streams. And the data collected provides a picture of that population; how many are present, what species, how fast are they growing, how old, and more.

And from that maze of information, decisions are made for the management of the body of water. Decisions that dictate the luck that people like you and I will have when we bring our rods and reels.

Dusk was settling as Mike Yeazle, Johannes' assistant, headed the pickup truck up the highway with the ponderous boat and trailer in tow. Our destination was a little shallow lake west of Minong; a lake which will remain nameless out of deference to the people that live and fish there.

"We haven't surveyed the lake for quite awhile. I think we'll find some really nice bluegills and crappies. I've been hearing some good reports on it," Johannes explained as we rode.

The last glow of sunset shimmered in the west as Yeazle backed the big rig into the water. Stars and the half slice of a moon peeked down from the dark sky. The wingbeats of the last duck of the day whistled overhead. Eerie white steam rose ghost-like from the water in the crisp air, and my insulated float coat already felt good.

Johannes backed the boat away from the landing, turned on its rows of bright headlights, and hit the switch on the AC generator. The unit coughed to life, and we were off toward the Big Dipper hanging over the northern horizon.

Yeazle and I would man the long-handled dip nets up front and capture the fish temporarily stunned in the electrical field between the electrodes. Slowly the boat moved along the shoreline.

"Take everything on this first pass," Johannes told us indicating that he wanted to collect fish from the smallest to the largest so as to get a good cross-section of the population.

And fish we got. Like popcorn exploding in a popper, they flitted and flashed in the underwater fairyland of submerged weedgrowth and brush. The ice forming on the boat's rails was forgotten as we scurried to capture bluegills, crappies, bass and northern pike to be deposited in a tank filled with water.

Halfway around the lake and the tank was black with fish. Johannes eased the boat onto the sandy shore to examine the catch. Already the fish had revived, swimming energetically.

A family of coyotes yipped back in the woods as we sipped a cup of coffee and munched a sandwich.

The measuring board and the scale came out. Each fish would be measured for length, weighed, and a tweezer of scales taken from its side. Yeazle and I would do the tallying as Johannes handled the fish.

"Bluegill seven point eight inches, six ounces. Northern twenty-four two, four pounds three ounces," Johannes chanted as the more than a hundred fish were counted and released unharmed over the side.

Then a second run back toward the landing. A trophy walleye. A thirty-inch plus northern. A large-mouth over five pounds.

"Don't bring that in the boat," Johannes yelled as I held up a dizzy muskrat.

And at midnight when the work was done; 110 northern, 28 bass, and a bundle of panfish had been examined.

"You saw a good productive lake. There's a well-balanced fishery. The distribution of northerns and bass through all size classes shows there's good reproduction. And the length and weight of the panfish indicates excellent growth," Johannes explained.

I felt good as Yeazle dodged the deer on the jackpine-rimmed road shoulders during the ride home. I felt good because I'd had a chance to fish with a couple professionals.

When can I go again, Stan? That's all I want to know.

Country Music

Country music, I heard some good stuff the other day. I heard it out ice fishing — my last trip for the season.

It's not unusual to hear country music out on the ice. In the dead of winter when people are driving on, it's fairly common to hear Willie Nelson floating on the cold air from a radio or tape deck.

I've been a country music fan as long as I can remember. Back when I was knee high to a grasshopper, I'd tag along behind my uncle Joe or Ted when they'd stop at Joe Wagner's Tap for some socializing. And while they rehashed the last Saturday night barn dance, they'd slip me a couple nickels for the juke box.

Drop a coin in the little slot, push a button, and out would come Gene Autry and "You Are My Sunshine" or the Andrews Sisters with the "Beer Barrel Polka." Great songs. Classics. You still hear them today.

The country music scene has seen some truly fine artists over the last fifty years. Take Eddie Arnold and his "Cattle Call" record, one of the outstanding vocal renditions of all times. Patsy Cline; the purest voice that's ever come down a country road. Who can forget her plaintive "Sweet Dreams" and "Honky Tonk Angel?"

Hank Williams with his "Cheatin' Heart!" And just the

other night I saw Roy Acuff celebrating his 80th birthday on the Grand Old Opry, belting out his immortal "Wabash Cannonball."

Anne Murray and Loretta Lynn, legendary artists of recent years.

And today? Well, I'm as much a fan as ever. Waylon Jennings and Merle Haggard are high on my list. But at the top are George Jones of the men and Reba McEntire for the ladies. McEntire is a great performer. Not only can she sing, but she's country through and through; and it shows.

Country music, the pulse beat of America. A cultural something that sets us apart from the other cultures in the world.

But back to my last day of ice fishing.

I look forward to the last days of March and the early days of April. That's when I like to chase the bluegills and crappies. I'm one of the last to hang up my jig poles.

The day was a good one, the spring sun pushing the snowbanks backwards. I headed for a little lake, drilled some holes, and settled in for some serious fishing. I had the whole place to myself; its quiet, its solitude.

And that's when the first notes of country music hit my ears. Off in the distance a couple crows sent their cawing across the stillness. Back in the woods a woodpecker nervously tapped out a tune on a dead tree stub. Country sound, and I liked it.

An hour of fishing; but I couldn't find the 'gills. And I decided to move on — halfway across the country to another little lake, one that's been very good to me.

I parked the pickup, gathered up my gear, and headed onto the slushy ice. And some more country music. Down the shore, a newly-arrived mourning dove coo-cooed a soft melody, lyrics that told that spring had arrived.

As I leaned over my fishing holes, the crescendo of music began to build. Open water was already showing on the south end of the lake, and there the musicians were tuning up. A few scattered chords at first. But as the sun settled behind the jack pines and the long shadows crept across the ice, the main act came on stage.

First the redwing blackbirds with a chorus deep back in the cattails. Then a pair of baritone mallards quacking, picking up the beat, adding volume. A splash of a beaver echoing in the dusk like the crash of a dummer's cymbal. Overhead a trio of woodducks cheeped in soprano unison.

And then the stars of the show! I heard their excited bugling as they raced across the water to get airborne, a quartet of Canada geese. Down the lake they came right to me, their voices harmonizing, serenading me as I sat in my front row seat, center stage.

A full moon, a yellow warm-looking moon, shone through the hardwoods casting a gentle spotlight glow on the stage. And a horned owl hooted its final mournful backdrop sound. The show was over.

And as I stepped off the ice, I realized I'd been privileged to listen to the greatest country music of all time. A super act, one that is played over and over.

Move over George and Reba. Step aside Minnie Pearl. That grand old lady of the outdoor opry, Grandma Nature, is making her bow.

Don't miss her performance. The country music she'll play will top the charts.

How Old Are Fish?

I caught the walleye last October. I felt the gentle tap as the fish picked up the jig-and-minnow bait. And as I set the hook, I knew it was no ordinary fish.

The walleye fought deep, bulldozing in circles just off the bottom; and I put all the pressure I dared on the six-pound line. Ever so slowly I worked the fish up, and my first glimpse of its white-tipped tail and its bronze sides told me it was a dandy.

With a feather touch on the reel handle, I brought the beauty to the surface, slipped the landing net under it, and brought it into the boat. I unhooked the jig from its lip and laid the prize on the yardstick screwed to the center seat of the boat; 26 1/2 inches it measured, close to seven pounds. A trophy in any walleye anglers book.

But how old was it? The age of fish has always interested me. And that night I placed a tweezer of scales from its side into an envelope.

The next day I stopped to see Stan Johannes, our local fish manager, and asked him if he would age the fish for me. A couple weeks later, back came his report. "The walleye you caught was at least twelve years old," his note said.

Twelve years! Now that's a long time for a critter to survive in a hostile environment. That meant that back in the spring of 1975 an egg had been laid and fertilized one spring night on a wave-washed gravel bar by a pair of honey-mooning walleyes.

A little fingerling had been born. A baby fish that had escaped hungry perch, diseases, and fisherman's baits for over a decade. That is, until I'd twitched that jig under its nose.

The aging of fish is a vital part of the management of fish populations. Age data is obtained in several ways. The most common method is to place a scale under a microscope. There annual growth rings can be observed; annuli they're called. The rings are very comparable to the annual rings of a tree.

But in very old fish, annuli become difficult to read with accuracy. Terry Margenau, a DNR research biologist told me, "We can be accurate up to about eight years. Then the annuli become packed."

Margenau went on to explain that biologists are now using sections of a spine from the dorsal fin of walleyes. "We've found fish in the St. Louis River which migrate from Lake Superior that are twenty years old." Fish from cold water tend to live longer lives.

Old fish are usually big fish. But not always. Factors other than age affect the growth of fish.

I visited with Howard Snow, another biologist. "Density of the population, or really the amount of food available per fish, is the most important determinent of fish growth. We used to think geographical differences, say between northern and southern Wisconsin, were a factor. But now we believe that density and food supply are more important," he said.

Stan Johannes gave me a chart which shows the average age of different species of fish by length here in northwest

Wisconsin. Following is some rounded-off ballpark information from his chart.

The walleye, our most sought game fish, reaches good size, say 16 inches, at about six years. But a trophy of 25 inches takes about twelve years.

Muskies, the king of sport fish, grows to legal length of 32 inches in about seven years. Yet thirteen years are required to produce a wall-hanger of 46 inches.

Northern pike hit keepable size of 22 to 24 inches in five or six years. But a 34-incher has to live ten years.

Bass, a sporty fish to many anglers, grow to a respectable 15 inches in six or seven years. But a braggin' hawg of 18 inches probably is ten years old.

Panfish? We think they grow like weeds. Not true. A decent bluegill eight inches long is also eight years old. And a foot-long crappie is ten.

Trout? A study of Eighteen Mile Creek up in Bayfield County, one of my summer hangouts, found that brown trout reach eleven inches after three summers of growth. But one that you have to bend to get in the creel, say 20 inches, is likely to be seven years old at least.

Growing an annual crop of fish in our lakes and streams is a big job; one that takes time and a ton of knowledge. Know-how about things from tiny eggs spawned in watery nurseries every April to annual rings on a fish scale under a microscope.

Like I said, my walleye last fall was no ordinary fish. Yet in a way it was. It had its life history written on its side.

A Hot Summer Night

A hot summer evening. What does one do on a hot summer night?

Well, years back when the kids were small, Momma and I would drive down to the beach for a swim. But no, not now. Beaches are too hard on the nervous system these days.

Or I could plunk myself down on a lawn chair out in the backyard in the shade of a big oak. But then, I've never been a sedentary-type person. I can take only so much sitting.

So I decide to go with one of my favorite escapes, to retreat to a trout steam. Retreat to where I can stand waist deep in cool water, to where I can forget and fight off the heat. Maybe I'll catch a fish or two. Maybe I won't. It really doesn't matter.

I drive into the narrow, rutted, tree-lined lane; on past the long-abandoned farm house and barn, and park the pickup. Rivlets of sweat trickle down the back of my neck as I slip into the chest-high waders. I feel like a plump bratwurst being prepared in a microwave.

A quarter-mile hike along the daisy-dotted old hayfield, and I find myself picking my way through the marsh grass and alder brush creek bottom. The stream couldn't look more inviting as I gingerly step off the bank into its cold water.

"An evening catch of Trout"

The shock of its coolness hits my legs first, then upwards through the rest of me. And like a light switch thrown; I am alone, immersed, isolated in my private, personal little world. This is the way to spend a hot summer night. The best way.

Nonchalantly, almost reluctantly, I begin to wade my way upstream. Not a breath of air stirs. The leaves of the alders, the swamp popples hang limp and lifeless. Through their canopy, patches of cloudless blue sky hang over the scene. Last-of-the-day shafts of sunlight pierce the openings to blend in a pattern of dusky shadows and surrealistic brightness.

Over and around the old beaver dam I cautiously ease. A good place to trip and fill the waders with mucky, inky water. I know because I've done it.

On to a sharp bend where the stream cuts deep against a high bank, a place where almost invariably I can take a fish or two. Like a blue heron steathily stalking its prey, I work myself into position. A good cast, and the nightcrawler-baited hook drops with barely a ripple on the water, inches from the overhanging marsh grass.

A gentle tap as a fish picks up the bait, then the aggressive rush of line as it runs deep back into the coolness under the bank. I set the hook and soon a fat, beautifully-speckled brook trout is plucked from the water.

I pause, light my pipe, watch its blue smoke curl in the air. I look, I listen, and I sense the wondrous world around me.

A dragonfly zips by on its four fragile wings chasing mosquitoes. A bullfrog croaks a throaty "ka-runk" so close that I should be able to see it. My eyes probe its weedy mudflat home. A multitude of song birds voice their melodies in the brushy green around me. Off in a distant pasture a cow moos.

On upstream I move against the gentle push of the stream's current. Overhead a pair of brilliantly-plumaged drake wood ducks swoosh by, so close that I can hear the rush of air through their wings.

Another favored pool where the stream eddys deep. The brown trout feels the sting of the hook, and is all over the pool, splashing frantically on the surface, then digging with all its might to reach the tangle of roots under the bank. But to no avail, and I add it to the brookie in the creel.

A narrow rocky run where the water runs swift. But it's unfishable. Beaver cuttings clutter its surface. Up on the bank to sneak my way to its upper scum-covered head. The crawler drifts lazily under the grey-green ooze, and the brown trout hungry from dozing all day in the dark shade snatches the bait. Some tricky maneuvering, and it too is dropped into the basket hanging from my hip.

The still evening air cools as I fish on; picking up a trout here, another there. On past the truck to one last hallowed hole.

Silently I slip around the clump of alders, and almost face-to-face a drinking red-coated deer explodes from the stream, sending water flying, whistling and snorting as it plunges out of sight into the gathering darkness.

The sun has long disappeared, and the first stars blink above me. Off in the woods a young coyote yips a greeting to the night. Tall pine trees stand silhouetted black against the lingering glow of the sunset.

A hot summer night has passed on a trout stream.

He Sure Fooled Me

The guy sure fooled me.

Like the pool hustler that flubs his first half-dozen shots in a game of eight ball, then runs the table! Like the card shark that sits in on a poker game and innocently asks if three aces beats a pair of jacks!

Only this guy did it with a fishing rod.

There were four of us, three amateurs and then this semi-pro, off on a walleye trip. First and foremost was Johnny Walker, from Hayward, and our leader.

Then Tommy Newcomb, an old fishing pal of Walker's, over from the Boulder Junction country of Vilas County to spend a couple days on our northwest lakes. A schoolteacher by trade and a fishing guide by avocation, he can do things with a fish pole too.

Next myself. But that doesn't count much.

And last was Dick Birkholz out of Woodruff, and the guy that snookered me real good with his walleye catching ability.

Whitefish Lake, over in the Stone Lake area of Sawyer County, would be our destination.

My rig was loaded and waiting when the three pulled up to the driveway. Two boats we'd use. Walker with Newcomb in his. Myself and Birkholz in mine.

"Dick Birkholtz and his Whitefish Lake Walleyes"

I'd met Birkholz once before, last October when Walker and I were on our annual trek over to Newcomb's place for a fall fishing outing. Dick had stopped in with his big lab for a break from a partridge hunt. Today we'd fish together. As we headed for Whitefish, he stoked up a battered corncob pipe. Two pipesmokers teamed up, a good start. As we rode, the talk drifted to trout fishing. He told me how he fly-fishes streams like the Ontonagon, the Paint and Cook's Run in the upper peninsula of Michigan. How he's fished the White River in Bayfield County and the Namekagon for twenty years.

We rapped about ruffed grouse hunting. About labs and German shorthairs and the pleasures of watching a good dog work.

And that's where I started to go wrong. I should have caught on. This was no ordinary outdoorsman. But he faked me out!

Maybe it was the way he talked, soft and slow. Maybe it was that corncob hanging over the grey beard. Maybe it was the floppy hat, or the baggy shirt worn tails out. Hey! The guy could have been a political science teacher down at the university. How was I to know he could catch fish?

I should have figured him out when we stopped for bait. Fathead minnows I wanted. Give me a fathead on a yellow jig for walleyes anytime. But not this guy. "Throw a dozen leeches in the pail," he says. Just a dozen. That's enough.

And as the boat headed across the water, I blew it again. I saw the wispy graphite rod. I noticed the spider-web-thin line packed on the ultra-light reel, the neat well-stocked tackle box. Things that should have warned me that here was no run-of-the-mill walleye fisherman.

I put the boat on a slow drift a cast away from the weed

edge. I watched as the man tied on a tiny leadhead jig, tipped it with one of his leeches, and began his work. With a feather touch he tickled the weeds, twitching the leech. Five casts maybe, and he was into his first fish, a solid three pounder. Then a couple of undersized walleyes, "puppies" Walker calls them. And I still didn't tumble. One keeper. A fluke probably.

A short run across the lake. "I've had action along here," I told him as he again methodically went about his business. With precision accuracy he dropped the leech-tipped jig alongside the underwater growth, working the rod tip like a magician's wand.

The light rod bowed and bucked. "A good fish," he said in that soft voice of his. I watched as he played the walleye, backing off on the reel handle at just the right instant, then putting the pressure back on. A strong three-pounder, I thought as I slipped the net under the fish.

On the next cast, a repeat. Another 22-incher. Two casts. Two good fish. The man was showing me the finer points now.

Yet he wasn't finished. By the time he'd used the last of that dozen leeches, he'd hung two more fine fish to fill his limit. And the stringer had some real heft as I lifted it into the boat.

The man had put on a symposium. How to catch walleyes on a hot summer day, it was called. A demonstration I'll remember long.

And I'll tell you one more thing! I'll never shoot pool with the guy.

Fish Chowder

Vern Hacker was a fisheries biologist. Vern Hacker was also a friend of mine. We first met when he was working for the old Wisconsin Conservation Department over at Oshkosh.

But Hacker was more than a grower of fish. He was a man with a mission. Believing that people were missing the boat when it came to preparing fish for the table, he wrote a book. Put out by the DNR in 1982, it's called "A Fine Kettle of Fish."

People go fishing for a lot of reasons. There's the purist dry fly trout angler who seeks the solitude of a quiet evening on a lonely, wild stream. Then there's the dyed-in-the-wool muskie chaser who's hooked on catching 'old fence post' or 'jingle jaws', evil-eyed monsters the size of torpedoes.

But the rank and file fishing fraternity enjoys the sport for two reasons. First, these middle-of-the-roaders just like being outside in the fresh air to relax and re-charge the batteries of life. And secondly, they like to hang a couple of walleyes or a mess of crappies over the side of the boat, then bring 'em home for a fish fry.

Having been raised the oldest of eight kids back in the Depression-era, I grew up with only one thing on my mind when I went hunting or fishing. And that was to bring something home for the table. Over the years, I've put exactly one fish, a muskie, on the wall.

But over those same years, we've eaten a lot of fish at our house. We like them. And Momma's become a world class fish fixer by my tastes. Hacker's book rests on her cookbook shelf there in the kitchen alongside Betty Crocker and the other pros.

Vern's book contains recipes contributed by people from all over the state. While he concentrates on promoting and changing the image of so-called "rough" fish, the recipes can be adapted to other species.

There are 38 pages of ways to cook fish; methods commonly used like frying, baking and broiling. Then lesser ways like boiling, canning, chowders and soups, pickling, smoking, steaming and poaching. He tells how to can fish, marinate; make sauces, loaves and even fish sausage.

One of Momma's favorite ways to serve fish is in a chowder. A number of good recipes are around. Milt Dieckman, for example, has perfected his secret "fish soup" formula almost to the point of it being world famous. And I tried another using cheddar cheese recently when I stopped at Bill Barton's house. My taste buds are still tingling.

But Vern Hacker's chowder ranks right up with the best. Many's the time Momma's brewed a batch, and we've had the neighbors over. The room goes eerily quiet when it's served. All one hears is, "Mmm! This is good!"

Here's Hacker's recipe. It makes three gallons, so you will require at least a 12 quart kettle.

<u>Fish Chowder</u>
4-5 pounds boned fish. (You can use walleye, bass, bluegill, perch, cod, almost any kind. The best, however, is

northern pike.) Cut the fish in pieces and put in boiling water (enough to adequately cover the fish). Cook until fish flake (approximately 10 minutes).

Remove fish — SAVE THE WATER THEY WERE BOILED IN.

5 pounds of good white potato Peel, quarter and slice thin. Rinse several times in cold water to eliminate excess starch.

2 large (3 inch) onions. Put them in blender with a little water. Reduce to mush.

1 3/4 tablespoons salt

Put potatoes, onions and salt in water the fish were boiled in (enough to cover potatoes, and about a quart extra. Boil until potatoes are soft. Do not pour off liquid.) With a potato masher, reduce about 3/4 of the potatoes to a puree.

Break the fish into small pieces, and add to the potatoes and liquid.

Add a 28 ounce can of whole tomatoes. (Put in blender to break up.)

Add a family size (26 ounce) can of Campbell's tomato soup.
Turn down the heat.

Add: 3/4 tablespoon black pepper
1/2 pound of butter

1 pint of half and half
1/4 pound soda crackers reduced to meal in blender (approx. 1 1/2 cups. Add gradually so they mix well.)

The chowder is a meal in itself. It freezes very well.

Anyone interested in Hacker's book can purchase a copy for $1.95 from: Bureau of Fish Management, DNR, Box 7921, Madison, Wis. 53707.

My wife and I own a treasured copy. Inside the cover on the fly page, there's a little note, you see. "With my very best regards, Vern;" it says.
It's special — like his chowder!

A Final Fling at the Walleyes!

There's six of them. Old friends, the youngest 58, the others well into their sixties. Add 'em up, and they've got well over 300 years of fishing experience.

And they're tough. Each year they gather in kind of a fraternal ritual for one last fling at the walleyes before the lake freezes over. Each year they congregate in a remote fishing camp near Boulder Junction over in Vilas County.

Include me and it made seven of us. For the past two years I've been honored with an invitation to join their inner circle.

I said they're tough. They have to be to withstand the rigors of November cold, snow, and ice.

"You're not really a dedicated walleye fisherman unless you fish the weekend before deer season," Tommy Newcomb, the leader of the clan, remarked. He's a master angler. I think he could catch walleyes in a gravel pit.

We fished out of his camp on Rice Creek upstream from Island Lake, part of the Manitowish chain of lakes. The camp has been in his family since 1926. It's got character.

Built of split cedar logs with peeled balsam fir poles for rafters, there's fishing and hunting lore written all over it.

Along the eves, rest collections of old-time fishing plugs and battered mallard and bluebill decoys. On the wall hangs a bobcat hide taken many years ago. By a wall stands an ancient steel Franklin-type fireplace that has cheered many an evening's bull session.

From the crossbeams hang gas lights to cast their pale, yellow, flickering glow. Water comes from a long-handled red pump out back. And off in the other direction stands an outhouse; from the door of which one gets a magnificent view of the tall white and norway pines that shield the place.

Dawn brought the rattle of Newcomb in the kitchen putting the coffee pot on, and out of our sleeping bags we rolled. No need to check the thermometer. Just layer yourself with long johns, wool shirts and pants. Then top it all off with insulated coats and windbreaker parkas. On the feet go heavy wool socks and felt-lined deer hunting boots.

The first light of day found us easing small boats down the shallow, stumpy creek. Around a bend and a flock of big-bodied mallards fresh out of Canada jumped from the icy water. In a pine, two eagles eyed us.

Then a show of a lifetime. From behind us, in glided six whistling swans, snow-white, majestic; to land on the water ahead. Tired from their migration flight, the birds allowed us to approach to within a hundred feet. Then with powerful wing beats slapping the water, they took to the air once more.

Newcomb cut the little six-horse motor's speed, and our boat crunched, scraped and rocked as we broke through the barrier of ice at the head of the lake. A healthy chop on the water told me the wind chill would be well below freezing. I dug a pair of brown cotton gloves from my float coat and proceeded to cut a forefinger from the one I'd cast with.

"Use eighth-ounce leadheads and a small fathead minnow," Newcomb instructed as he dropped the anchor. Two casts and I felt the soft tap as a fish picked up the bait. Dropping my rod tip, I gave the fish a few seconds; then leaned into the hook set. A brief battle, and Newcomb slipped his net under the three-pound walleye, the first fish of the day.

Next, Newcomb into a good fish, and good-natured joshing from the other boats.

Into the morning we fished. Spray froze on the gunwales of the boat. Monofilament lines thickened as ice encased them, clogging the guides on our rods. The frigid wind whipped parka hoods from our heads.

Except for a lunch break, all day we toughed it out. And when the boats were slid onto the snow-covered shore at the cabin; plump, heavy-shouldered walleyes were dropped into a white plastic pail, enough to assure that everyone would have a couple meals of fillets to take home.

By the second morning, the weather had changed. Gone was the bright, windy, sunny cold; replaced with a sodden overcast sky that promised snow. And by mid-morning the white stuff descended, melting and slicking our raingear.

As the weather changed, so did the walleyes. Finicky, it took a feather touch on the leadheads to entice a fish to hit.

"Come 3:30, I'm ready to hang it up," Newcomb called across the water. When the appointed time arrived, we were all ready to pack it up.

As we headed in, four otters fished and played at the edge of the shelf ice rapidly forming from the banks of the creek. Past the beaver lodges and old duck blinds we eased. A muskrat cut a watery vee as it headed to a weedbed for supper.

At the camp fishing tackle was unloaded, motors removed from their transoms, and the boats skidded into the boat house.

The sinewy six had met. And another open water walleye fishing season was over.

"November Walleye Fishermen, Tom Newcomb and Lyle Henschel"

Fish House Fishing

It's a quiet little community; a nice neighborhood, well-planned with wide curving streets. The lots are spacious, occupied by single-story dwellings; the architecture of which blends nicely. Here and there TV antennaes sprout.

What struck me as different was the flat terrain and the absence of trees, sort of like Kansas in the winter time. But you can't have everything when you build a town on the frozen surface of a lake.

Wigwam Bay Estates, I called the place, a picturesque name if I ever heard one. And the best thing about the place is that it's all zoned "Fishing."

I'm talking about the village of fish houses on Mille Lacs Lake near Garrison, Minnesota where Bill Barton and I resided for three days and two nights recently. Our home was "The Huberty Hilton," a slate-blue cabin on skids, so-named by me for its owner.

Fish houses are big business on Mille Lacs. Ron Nelson, who operates The Wigwam Inn and campground on the west shore, takes care of 100 fish houses; some his own, others belonging to people like Huberty. Nelson explained that the 132,520 acre lake has between 4,000 and 5,000 houses on it each winter.

Barton's and my adventure actually began last October.

"Bill Barton lands a five pound Walleye"

Some Minnesota friends had come over to join us on a muskie fishing expedition. And in our fishing talk, Mille Lacs had come up. Over the years, I'd heard about its excellent walleye fishing, and I'd said I'd like to try the lake. "Why don't you come over and use our fish house?" they'd replied. Now there was a second reason. I'd never experienced living in a fish house. It'd be something interesting, different. So in early January the phone calls were made.

And as Nelson unlocked the door of the Hilton, I looked around. Carpeted floor, a propane gas furnace, four bunks, a three-burner gas plate to cook on. Include the heated biffy down the ice road, and we had almost all the comforts of home.

In the corners at the ends of our bunks were four holes drilled in the ice, the water glowing a pale green. On the wall above each hole hung what's known as "rattle reels," large spools holding the lines. Hang a fathead minnow on the hook, drop it down the hole, and you're in business. When a fish hits, bells inside the reels ding-a-ling. Ingenious!

I was barely unpacked, yet Barton had his lines down. One a rattle reel, the other a rod baited with a jigging spoon tipped with a minnow. "I've got one already!" he hollers. "And it's a good one!"

I leaped for the gaff hook and crowded in to give him a hand. And in a minute or two; the biggest fish of the trip, a walleye a tad under 25 inches and five pounds, laid flopping on the carpeted floor.

Except for a couple of runs to shore, we fished 24 hours a day. We fished while we ate, and we fished while we slept. So what if the indoor-outdoor thermometer on the wall read below zero outside. Inside it read 75 degrees as the gas furnace toasted the place.

"Maybe I won't want to go south this winter after this!" Barton laughed.

And after dark, we switched on the four little battery-operated lights on the ceiling, set up a card table and broke out the cribbage board til bedtime.

Mille Lacs has got to be one of the outstanding bodies of water in the upper midwest. "A few years ago it was called the dead sea," Nelson told me. "But we got together and turned it over to the DNR. Now it's managed as an experimental lake. And the programs are working."

The lake has a population of 1,100,000 catchable walleyes and gives up 275,000 of them to sport fishermen each year. Special regulations apply. For example, the bag limit is six, but only one can be larger than 20 inches. Then for a period in May and June, night fishing is restricted. Both regulations are intended to protect the larger female walleyes, the heavy spawn producers.

The lake also has an excellent yellow perch fishery. And that's what gave us most of our action. Walleye fishing in January is marginal on most waters.

On our last day, Nelson decided to move his houses to a perch reef. "If you guys want to catch perch, come on out," he told us.

Well now, Barton is a perch addict, and Nelson's words were like putting raw hamburger in front of my German shorthair. And across the ice for two miles we followed Nelson's trail.

It may take Barton awhile to locate a school of perch. But he'll drill holes until he does. And he did. For the last afternoon, we had excellent fishing; catching heavy-bodied perch up to a foot long. And when the time came to head home, two pails were heavy with fish.

I hate to admit it, but Barton outfished me something fierce. He had the hot hand.

But not on the cribbage board. He couldn't hit a sixteen hand for sour apples.

I cleaned his clock for 87 cents!

Prof Perch Calls the Shots!

The words echoed across the frozen expanse of ice and snow. "Are you having fun yet?"

And back came the answer, tainted with a bit a sarcasm, "I'm having a ball!"

School was in session. Class had been called. Professor W. Perch Barton had taken four of us, his students, on a field trip; on an academic exercise to educate us in the finer points of perch fishing.

"Old Prof Perch," as I call our respected and beloved tutor, had brought us to the wilds of northern Minnesota. To Lake Winnibigoshish, or Big Winnie as it's usually known.

Prof Perch is the head of the Department of Perch Sciences and Piscatorial Arts at Perch University. P.U., as I refer to this hallowed institution of lower learning, conducts its affairs in the basement of the old educator's home near Stone Lake. From its fish scale covered walls, have come some of the least talented, most unqualified members of the perch fishing profession in the world.

"Listen up, you turkies!" the good prof began his lecture, holding up a fishing rod. "Today I shall demonstrate to you how to turn this tiny piece of innocent looking graphite into a deadly weapon. Are there any questions?"

From the back of the class, a voice timidly spoke up.

"Prof Perch, what's for supper?"

His dignity severely impinged, the aged scholar was obviously deeply wounded. "You see," he said, a twinge of disgust in his tone. "That's what I mean! You guys stop listening to me and we're through as a fishing team! Now get your tails in gear and get those Swedish pimples in the water."

And dutifully we obeyed, dropping our hooks to research the perch population of Big Winnie.

We tried. We gave it our best shot.

Overhead a frigid clear blue sky stretched from horizon to horizon. Overnight a massive cold air mass had slid down upon us from Canada. The Arctic high pressure system had sent the thermometer plummeting. From the leading edge of the cold air, a twenty-mile-an-hour northwest wind blew, blasting us with wind chills of twenty below at best.

It was cold. Believe me! Unrelenting, brutal, penetrating, creeping invisible cold that seeped through the thick layers of heavy clothing we were wearing. Grueling, grinding cold that stiffened muscles and turned faces beet-red. Gnawing cold that split lips and finger knuckles. Cold that dulled the emotions, sending thoughts of frostbite and hypothermia through my mind.

For four days we fought the battle. And when it was over, the weather had won. We caught perch, but nothing like we should have. And our price in pain had been high.

The saving grace in the whole picture was Bob Kline's snug, warm cabin back on shore where we thawed out each night. Kline is the owner of the Nodak Lakeview Lodge, our headquarters. Centered in the moose and timber wolf country of the Chippewa National Forest, Kline's resort hosts many Wisconsin fishermen each year.

I talked with Kline about Big Winnie. The lake has some

70,000 acres of water, he said. It produces big muskies and northerns, excellent walleyes, and jumbo perch. "Fishing has been good when the weather's been good," he told me.

This winter has been unusual. Early snowstorms had dumped a thick layer of snow on the lake, causing slush to form and making the plowing of his many miles of ice roads difficult. Then came the cold February that tightened up the lake but discouraged all but the hardiest fishermen.

Yet someone once said to me that there's no such thing as a bad fishing trip. I agree. As a student of Old Prof Perch, I won't measure our recent trip by the number of fish I caught.

Instead it'll stick out in my memory as the time I fought the most punishing weather I've ever fished in. I'll remember it for the expertise the old teacher demonstrated in catching big eelpout, the ugliest fish that swims, and his promise to put on an eelpout boil when summer rolls around.

And I'll remember how the old professor placed his power auger upright in a hole in the ice and allowed it to freeze in so solidly that it took four of us a half hour with a second auger, an axe and a spade to free it.

Yup, the old prof may goof up, make a mistake once in awhile.

But so what, we love the guy.

Of Rhubarb and Walleyes!

My Uncle Bill was pure country, full of the cliches of his time. Things like "Hoo Boy! There'll be frost on the pumpkin tonight." Or "Think the rain will hurt the rhubarb?" And his memory came back to me as I stood in the backyard checking out the morning.

Opening day of the fishing season, yet there stood the rhubarb sprouting, its red stems and unfurling green leaves trimmed, fur-like, with ermine snow. Nearby the swelling buds of a lilac bush looked pitiful swaying in the cold northwest gale. Over in the pine trees, a robin weakly chirped, like it was hurting, in deep pain.

Opening day for what, I thought. Fishing? I've seen better weather for the opening of the deer season.

But I had a date to keep. In a couple hours I was scheduled to join Johnny Walker on a little boat landing "somewhere in northern Wisconsin." And I'd be there come wind, hail, sleet or snow.

The pickup was packed. The night before I'd stowed my gear. But after testing the weather, a prudent concession to old age was made. Down from a nail on the garage wall came my heaviest ice fishing coat, one that has shielded me from the fiercest of cold.

As I eased out of town on the main highway, the first

thing I noticed was the slow pace of the traffic. And I saw why. The road was slippery, icy in places. Winter driving in May!

And as I made the turns onto the side roads to the boat landing, the car tracks on the snow-covered blacktop and gravel became fewer and fewer. One track into the landing, one car with an empty boat trailer parked. And as I pulled a pair of rain pants over my Sorrel boots, that fisherman beached his boat.

I walked over to talk with him. He was quitting, he said. "Haven't had a bite. I'm froze, my nightcrawlers are froze, my leeches are froze! My hands are so cold I couldn't even change baits!" Things sounded worse than I feared.

And where was Walker? A half-hour wait and in he pulls. "Been working on this stupid motor. Yesterday it started right off. Today it won't. Must be some ice in the gas line!" Things weren't getting any better.

But Johnny's an old guide. He's used to adversity. "I'll row," he said. "We'll work the shoreline. The walleyes should be in tight." And as the boat drifted downwind from the landing, I got ready for my first cast of the '89 season.

"Put these on," John said, "They'll help keep your hands dry." And he handed me a pair of white latex throw-away surgical gloves. I had doubts, but I slipped the little gloves on. They felt surprisingly good, and I held my hands up for an inspection. "Would you like an examination?" I asked, a little humor effort in what was so far a humorless situation.

And we began to fish, casting our old standby walleye lures, jigs tipped with minnows into the froth-flocked waves splashing against the rock-strewn shoreline. Five minutes, and John is into the first fish. A fish that fought deep, so powerfully that he never raised it enough to see what it was.

A mammoth walleye? A big muskie? And into a submerged treetop it dove, breaking the line.

Then the first walleye landed, a nice two-pounder by John. One on the stringer. We'd not be skunked. But the erratic bouncing of the boat tested my jig fishing patience. In my brain an old fishing instinct stirred, and I switched to an artificial lure. And the move made the day.

First, a deep running new bait called the Shadrap. Maybe ten casts and two nice walleyes caught on it. And John switched to one too. Slowly, we worked the rocky shore, anchoring to hold the boat, picking up a fish or two at each stop.

A shallower sandy spit, and I changed to a floater silver Rapala. "I've got another," I called, "And it's a good one," as I played a fish, expecting a nice walleye to come to the surface. But up came a bass, one that would go a good four pounds, a spawning female; and I eased the hook from its lip and dropped it back into the lake.

Suddenly the day seemed warmer, the cold not so cold, the wind not so windy. Our mood mellowed as we added walleyes to the stringer. We listened as a pair of Canada geese honked by overhead. We watched the swallows skim the waves picking miniscule insects, the sandpipers pecking at bugs on the rocks along the bank.

When it was all over, ten nice walleyes, our limits, were swimming on stringers alongside the boat. A day that had promised the worst, had produced the best.

The snow hadn't hurt the fishing. And it didn't hurt the rhubarb either.

A Big Trout

"Just say no!" is a buzz phrase these days. When it comes to going fishing, I have a hard time saying no.

Today's tale involves two fishing trips. One for walleyes, the other for trout; both influenced by a gully-washer rain we had recently.

A partner and I were working a little lake early that evening, trying to locate the walleyes. Around us swirled black clouds, dumping showers on us. But snug in our rain suits, the weather was nothing we couldn't handle.

But then the sky fell in. Lightning flashed, thunder boomed, and a torrent of rain sent us to shore. For an hour we sat in the pickup, waiting for the storm to pass. Finally, we had to give up, load the boat and head home.

Yet as I'd sat there watching the downpour, my mind had slowly turned to trout fishing. Nothing heats my fishing blood more than a good two-inch soaker. That's when the big brown trout come out to play.

Sure, the rain had ruined the walleye outing. But turn a problem into a solution, a negative into a positive. And as I parked the boat in the garage, down from the wall came the waders, and the trout rod. The next morning at daylight, I'd be on The Beautiful Lady, my favorite trout steam.

Maybe I wouldn't catch a fish. Just my being there, when

she was alive and bursting with energy, would be enough.

The world was half-daylight, half-darkness as I slid into my waders, silent but for the songs of early-rising birds, and the "clump" of my boots on the path through the woods. To the east, the first shafts of sunrise painted the new green tops of the aspens. The freshly-bathed earth had the squeeky clean smell of a grandson just out of the bathtub.

What a morning to be out, I told myself. And as I topped the ridge, the Lady's first soft murmur came to me, music that became a crescendo as I dropped down into her valley.

She had water! Oh, but she had water! There she was, roaring and wrenching, showing her muscle. And as I stepped from the bank; the power, the strength of her current told me that this was a day to watch my step. One booted toe hooked under a rock or a sunken log, and she'd dump me but good.

We'd be alone, the Lady and I. Just the two of us to romance together as we have for better than twenty years; a love affair few can understand or appreciate. Except for the mosquitos chewing on my ears and the wood ducks wooshing by overhead, we'd be alone.

The first fish, a foot-long brown, came too quickly, too easily. As I dropped it into the creel, I felt a twinge of regret. I wanted to fish, not necessarily to catch fish, to savor the morning.

And I moved on; slowly picking my way upstream, cautiously testing the bottom for sure footing with each slow step, as the Lady tugged at my legs. Around pools too deep to wade. Across the flooded meadow where the wet yellow marsh marigolds glistened in the sunlight.

Small trout caught and released. A fair brookie added to the creel. Then three more nice browns, and I was one short

"A nice Trout from the Beautiful Lady"

of my five-fish brown trout limit. Little did I realize the hand that fate was about to deal to me.

I know the place well. It's a deep narrow run, one that I can barely fish in normal water without going over my waders. Today, it ran five, maybe six, feet deep. Through the flooded mucky swamp, I eased to its edge. The nightcrawler splashed upstream, settled into the dirty water, and drifted toward me. I felt the tug, watched my line slide under the marsh grass-covered bank. And I set the hook. This would be no ordinary trout.

Deep and powerfully it fought, so hard that I put all the pressure I dared on the line to turn the fish as it plunged to escape into the tangle of roots and snags. The water swirled and boiled as it battled. A glimpse of its golden sides, its huge head, and I found myself wondering just how big it was.

And how would I land it? One false move and into the drink I'd go. The only way, I decided, was to play the fish until it was totally exhausted, and take my chances of losing it.

Slowly, gradually, the trout tired, riding to the surface. With its hook-jawed mouth agape, I eased it cross-current toward me. And with a lucky grab, I grasped its broad shoulders and lifted it from the water. Three pounds, six ounces it was to weigh, a tad under twenty inches.

The day with The Beautiful Lady was done. Once again, she'd been good to me.

The Sweet Corn Trip

We always called it the "sweet corn trip." Every year about now, when the sweet corn was ripening, Bill Waggoner would get us together for a fling at the trout.

Waggoner was an organizer of men, a good one. His plan was simple. Get a dozen of us together, catch some trout, and cook 'em up with a batch of sweet corn.

But there was more motive to it than that. Bill figured if people played well together, they'd work well together. So he recruited us, people that worked together in a loose affiliation – men from the county court house, the state patrol, the DNR, and others. And we'd go fishing.

On the morning of the appointed day, we'd gather as the dawn's first light crept in from the east; meeting to exchange hushed "good mornings"; to shuffle fishing rods, waders and creels from car trunk to car trunk.

And north we'd head along Highway 63 to the Grandview and Delta country where the White River and its feeder streams waited for us.

Bill was in command. Each fisherman knew exactly what stretch of stream he was to fish, where to begin, where to end.

Hugh Smith, you take the Eighteen Mile south of old 63. Bill Dougherty, you fish the Long Branch from the bridge to the cabin. Bill Albright, you walk down to where the Eighteen Mile comes in and fish back to the bridge. Becker, you're on the Eighteen Mile from the Swamp Road up to Grandview.

There'd be a breakfast stop at Hayward, fortification for the effort ahead; the work of bucking the current of a cold stream, picking through alder thickets, and swatting mosquitos. Over the ham and eggs, the table talk flowed; stories of past trips when big browns darted from undercut banks to smack French spinners and Panther Martins.

And questions for Lloyd Potterton. Lloyd was always in charge of the sweet corn. "Was it ripe?" "Are you sure there's enough?" "Boy, there's nothing better than Seneca Chief!"

Then north through Seeley, Cable and Drummond. And one by one, we'd slip into our waders and hit the water.

I remember the first trip I made with Waggoner. Bill put me on the Long Branch at what he called "the motorcycle hole," so named for an old motorcycle parked there in the woods. Anxious to get fishing, I stepped into the stream, waved him what I thought was a good-bye, and began to cast.

Well, I hadn't gone fifty feet when I wrapped my brand-new spinner around an overhanging branch. There I stood belly-deep trying to free it. And there, next to it, hung one of the biggest yellow jacket nests I've ever seen. Gingerly, I worked to tease the spinner free; all the while praying I wouldn't disturb the hornets. If I did, I'd be in big trouble.

And out of the brush came a hearty laugh. I turned, and there stood Bill, enjoying every second of my predicament. Memories are made of such.

By late afternoon, we'd be out of the woods, leg sore from

easing over slippery rocks and crawling around log jams. New tales would be spun and big browns proudly displayed. And we'd adjourn to Hugh Smith's deer shack or Mike Linton's farm for supper.

From Potterton's car would come a burlap bag of Seneca Chief, and green husks flew as the ears were peeled. A couple of Coleman camp stoves would be gassed and lit. On would go a big kettle of water; and when it was steaming, in went the golden corn.

Hugh Smith was the chef. Into his black, cast-iron skillets went a layer of bacon, makings for bacon sandwich appetizers. Then into the sizzling grease would be dropped the floured and seasoned trout.

And over the scene, hung a delicious, delectable aroma, a blend of smells that titillated the taste buds and honed hunger pangs pleading for relief after a hard day in the fresh air.

Talk about good eating! Let Smith and Potterton announce that chow was on, and beware of flying elbows. Butter dripped from chins and fingers. And stripped corn cobs and bared fish skeletons piled high.

We'll be taking the sweet corn trip again one of these days. After all, we've been making it for over twenty years now. And we can't let a tradition like that end.

Bill Waggoner won't be with us.

But then, I might just hear a hearty laugh from somewhere off in the distance.

And I'll know who it is.

The Shorelunch Scientist!

Milt Dieckman cooks a mean shorelunch! I know — I've sat in on a few.

A good shorelunch is more than just a meal outside. It's an outdoor adventure of sorts, an experience long remembered.

I've been fortunate. Over the years, as I've rammed around on more lakes, rivers and streams than one man probably has a right to, I've watched some mighty fine outdoor cooks in action. And in atmospheres that the best of eating places couldn't duplicate.

Picture if you will, a lonely island with pine trees standing tall, the wind softly sighing through needled branches high above. Blue smoke sifts lazily skyward as a campfire of driftwood snaps and crackles. Against a rock-strewn shore, gentle waves lap and splash, playing background music. Perhaps a white-headed eagle floats majestically on motionless wings in a blue sky overhead. And from a distant bay, a loon sends an eeerie melodious yodel.

Imagine that if you can, and you'll have a fair start toward understanding what shorelunches are all about. They're more than a means to satisfy hunger pains. They're food for the soul as well.

My first shorelunch came many years ago on a fishing trip

"Milt Dieckman prepares a Shorelunch"

to Canada. A guide did the honors, serving up walleye fillets on a barren bedrock spit jutting into the lake. I was young; I loved the outdoors; but above all, I had a good appetite. And I'll never forget the sight and the smell of that meal cooking in his pots and pans over that open fire.

Since that first experience, I've shared similar campfires with a number of people, men who could perform magic with a spatula. An example. Years back, a group of us always opened the fishing season on Nelson Lake. Come noon, on a balsam fir-covered point, Tony Jelich would do the cooking, broiling steaks so tender they'd almost melt in your mouth.

Bill Barton's no slouch either. I join him each winter for some ice fishing. Let him break out his little portable grill at noon on frozen Whitefish Lake up in Ontario, unwrap his venison steaks, and you just know something great is about to happen.

Then there are guys like Bob Dreis, Jim Bishop, George Petry and Barry Nielsen. I ate some of their fixins this summer. People are still talking about the strawberry shortcake that Petry topped his fare off with.

But I think it's safe to say that the high guru of shorelunch cookers is Milt Dieckman. He's earned that reputation. Milt has made a science out of shorelunches. Just watching him perform is worth the price of admission.

Dieckman's dinners begin the day before. That's when he plans his menu, collects his "makins," and assembles the array of equipment he'll need.

There's fresh lettuce and cucumbers for a salad from his garden, wild rice from the private stock he puts up each year to be soaked. Then a trip to the store for three or four kinds of beans and a supply of potatoes. And frozen crappie and bluegill fillets thawed, ingredients for his famed "fish soup."

The next day finds his boat loaded to the gunwales. There's a wooden locker cached with the lesser supplies, things like spatulas, gloves, and seasonings. And a giant two-foot-across frying pan; two rubber duffle bags laden with smaller pans, a bean kettle, and an ancient coffee pot. A battered steel grill completes the inventory.

Over all the gear, hangs an aura, an image of shorelunches past, the sides and bottoms of the utensils blackened by countless campfires permeating a sense of permanence and constancy.

And the man himself adds to the scene. There he'll stand; quietly laboring, opening cans, emptying their contents, mixing and stirring, all in a routine he's performed hundreds of times as he's prepared meals for the mightiest and the meekest.

There he'll stand, an age-old floppy felt guide's hat on his head, the tails of a time-traveled flannel shirt hanging loose, dispensing bits of subtle philosophy about the outdoors and life in general, all while his bacon is sizzling and his soup is simmering.

He fed 42 of us one day last year on an island in the Chippewa Flowage. Now that's a fair crowd to have over for supper under the best of kitchen conditions. But feed 42 grown men a meal they won't soon forget, one cooked over a campfire out in the boondocks; well, that takes some doing, a real touch of class.

And that's why I call him the king of the shorelunch cooks.

We Struck Out!

Back in his big-league baseball days, Tom Poquette could handle a curve ball pretty well. Let a pitcher make a mistake, say hang one out over the plate, and the odds were good that Poquette would rattle the ball off the centerfield fence.

But now the ball park was different. We were fishing, not playing baseball. And the fish were throwing the curves.

Three of us; Poquette, Joe Weiss, and I had joined forces to do battle with the northern pike. There we stood, huddled in heavy clothing against snow slanting down before a brisk wind, on one of our favorite pike lakes; our tipups spread over an acre of ice that has always been productive territory.

But the fish weren't having any of us. When fish bite, I've learned, the talk of fishermen tends to stick pretty much to fishing. Excitement generated by flags tripping skyward or bobbers dipping down holes.

But when the fish don't cooperate, then the conversation tends to drift. Just about anything's fair game...politics, old war stories, what's wrong with the world; you name it.

And that's where we found ourselves. The pike were tossing a no-hitter against us. And to take our minds off how bad we were getting beat, we talked.

I'd met Poquette once before. He'd come up from Eau Claire to join Joe Weiss for a day of musky fishing on Big

Sisabagama. And at shorelunch time, they'd joined the rest of us for some socializing. The two are lifelong friends, born in Eau Claire and growing up there doing things boys do. Like riding their bikes over to the Chippewa River to fish for carp, as Joe reminisced with a laugh.

Boys grow into men, however. And they did. Joe, he learned to fly airplanes. Today he's a pilot for a major airline, flying people to all parts of the world.

Tom learned to play baseball. He learned well, and his skills carried him to the major leagues where he played the outfield for the Kansas City Royals, Boston Red Sox and Texas Rangers for several years back in the 1970's.

And since those active playing days, he's become a manager of minor league teams in the Kansas City Royals organization.

Having knocked around baseball's minor leagues myself a bit back in my youth, I can vouch to the fact that it's not the most pleasant life, what with long, hot, overnight bus rides and cheap hotels.

But Poquette has paid his dues, and he's moved up the ladder. Last year, for instance, he managed Memphis in the Class AA Southern League, one of the fastest minor leagues in the country. And this year, he's moving up to Omaha where he'll serve as batting coach. Omaha's in the Class AAA American Association, one notch below the majors.

"No more bus rides," he commented. "Now I get to fly."

I asked if he has some good prospects coming along, players that will make the parent Kansas City club someday. There were, he said, and mentioned several names, young players he's helped to develop. A "Triple A" league, he said, also serves as a reservoir for players that can be called up when needed, as when a major leaguer becomes injured.

In the off season, as now, Poquette likes to hunt and fish. And as expected, our talk drifted to that too. Tom owns a cabin up near Barnes, where Weiss joins him. And some good-natured razzing about some of their deer hunting exploits.

Seems one year, over in the Ounce River country, Tom drove a swamp to try to push a deer out to Joe. And he did. "Biggest buck I ever saw!" Joe chuckled. "At least twelve points!"

"Yeah, and you missed him!" Tom reminded him. "That I did," Joe admitted. "At point blank range too! Could have almost reached out and touched him with the gun barrel! But at least I didn't have to shoot one that was blind in one eye like you did."

So the afternoon passed. The venison steaks Weiss broiled over charcoal to juicy, tender perfection were polished off, topped with a jar of cold, crispy dill pickles. Dessert was a big scoop of good conversation.

Nary a pike was caught. Nary a flag went up.

The fish had struck us out.

Wilderness Walleyes

The rack of bull moose horns hanging over the log cabin's door set the mood for the trip. The timber wolf put a fitting close to it.

Four of us were off on one of our annual ice fishing expeditions to Whitefish Lake in southern Ontario.

The drive through northeastern Minnesota, along Lake Superior's ruggedly beautiful shoreline, gets our juices flowing. But when we turn off the main highway onto the twisting road that winds its way into the Canadian bush, that's when the heart really begins to pump.

There's an aura about the country; its vastness, its emptiness, its bedrock cliffs, its wall-to-wall spruce and balsam forests, that tells us we've left the real world behind.

And there in the woods stands the snug little cabin, probably somebody's hunting shack, with the moose horns over the door. Its sight marks the dividing line between civilization and wilderness. A door closes in my mind on life as I know it today, and another opens to an atmosphere that has existed, almost unchanged, since time began.

Like the moose horns and the timber wolf and the wilderness, the trip was a study in contrasts. We'd come to Whitefish to sample its outstanding yellow perch fishing. We'd been there before in the past. Never have the perch failed to cooperate. But not this trip.

Maybe the hex began when we pulled out of my drive-way, and for some mysterious reason the CB radios in the two pickups refused to talk to one another.

Maybe the jinx continued when we missed a directional sign as we entered the highway interchange south of Duluth and got separated. "Malfunction Junction" I call the spaghetti-like complex of exit ramps. We've been lost there before.

The two incidents should have signalled to us that something was amiss on the trip. For three days we struggled to get the perch to bite, trying every technique and trick and lure in our tackle boxes to entice the fish. Bill Barton and I spent the better part of a day travelling the 24-square mile lake, fishing old familiar spots that had produced on previous trips, drilling holes through the foot-thick ice in new places, talking to other fishermen.

But to no avail. At the end of our three-day stay, the perch catch barely filled a five-gallon pail.

The walleye fishing was the saving grace. Not outstanding, but good. Whitefish Lake, in addition to its perch population, contains high numbers of walleyes. We caught the fish on everything from tiny teardrop jigs tipped with waxies to tipups baited with six-inch sucker minnows.

Most of the walleyes ran small, from one to three pounds. The lake has a tremendous population in that size class right now, a good omen for the future. Except for a few for a couple meals back at our cabin at John Lark's fishing camp, the rest were released.

Two fish, however, were outstanding. Both Barton and Joe Zanter caught eight-pounders, trophy walleyes to be sure. And we heard of others caught that were larger, one that weighed in at over ten pounds.

I like to jig for walleyes with artificial lures, baits like the ice Rapala and the Swedish pimple. There's something about the "thunk" of a fish socking the lures that I really enjoy. And the walleyes give me a lot of action on my light rod.

But there's more to a fishing trip than catching fish.

A special thrill came one morning while Barton and I were exploring for perch. Busy concentrating on my fishing, I hadn't noticed the commotion on the ice a mile away. But Barton's keen, experienced eye for the unusual in the outdoors had.

"Take a look at this," he said, walking over to me and handing me a pair of binoculars. "Looks like a timber wolf over there on the ice."

I fixed the glasses on the black dot, and the wolf jumped into my vision, its huge head, bushy tail characterizing the animal. Surrounding the animal was a half-dozen ravens, and periodically the wolf would rush the birds, sending them scattering.

"He's feeding on something," Barton said. And for a half hour, we took turns watching. Finally, after satisfying its hunger, the wolf nonchalently, majestically trotted off to the wooded shoreline.

So the perch fishing had been a disappointment! I'd seen a timber wolf in the wild, a rare treat, the highlight of the trip.

And that's what makes fishing in the Canadian wilderness such a soul-satisfying experience.

A Kind and Gentle Man

He was a kind and gentle man – long before kinder and gentler became a standard for a nation.

His name was Sheldon. But we never called him that. In our family he was always Grampa Wight. And our kids remember him best as the man that would sit with them for hours, back in their youth, playing checkers or working a jigsaw puzzle.

He's been gone now for many years. Yet, his memory lives on. It came back to me the other day, the day before Christmas, as I knelt on one knee in the snow of a frozen lake rigging one of my ice fishing lines.

"Grandpa, where did you get these tipups?" my eight-year-old grandson, Ben, had asked as he eyed the strange contraptions.

"Ben, Grandma's father made them for me," I answered matter-of-factly. And suddenly, like a bolt of electricity flashing through my brain, the full impact of the moment hit me. I paused for a few seconds, pondering its significance, before I continued.

"He was your great-grandfather," I added. "And he gave me these tipups forty years ago today, on Christmas Eve, as a Christmas present."

The story behind that gift had begun one night a year earlier. I was a young college student; and fate had chosen to place a young lady in the chair behind me of my political science course. A young lady with freckles on her face and auburn hair that hung in bangs over her forehead. A young lady that today I affectionately refer to as "Momma" in this column.

"Hello," she'd said as I sat down. "Hello," I'd answered. And as class closed, I asked if I could walk her home.

There, for the first time, I met her family; the kind and gentle man, her mother, and eventually her two brothers.

The twice-a-week walks after political science became a routine, and slowly but surely I found myself being drawn into the young lady's family. By their openness, their friendly banter, by the great pies her mother baked, thick wedges of which she served to send a skinny, hungry college kid on his way.

We found a lot in common. Her folks had been farm people and knew some of my kinfolks. Her two brothers were both veterans of World War II, as I.

But the strongest glue of all was fishing. They were a fishing family. And I gazed enviously at the huge muskie hanging on the wall that Doug, the young lady's brother had caught. I listened to the tales the family told of their summer camping trips to Beaver Dam Lake near Cumberland, on the kind and gentle man's one week's vacation from his job as a machinist each year.

We began to fish together. Doug teaching me to use a fly rod, to lay a dry fly over a bed of spawning bluegills. And the kind and gentle man and I standing on the ice on winter days.

And that's where the tipups were born. Back then, tipups were handmade. In my mind, I'd dreamed of the perfect tipup. Casually, I'd described it to the man and forgotten the incident.

Christmas Eve of 1949 found me once more gathering with the young lady's family. Under the brightly lighted tree, the gifts laid. One by one, they were passed to be opened.

The kind and gentle man handed me a lumpy package, one he'd wrapped himself I'm sure. I had no idea what was in it, but as our eyes met, his told me that it was a gift from the heart.

Inside were ten beautifully crafted ice fishing tipups, each made of brass and German silver, manufactured to precision by the hands of a master machinist. Reels that spun as if they were mounted on jeweled bearings. Solder joints neat and tight. Ten tipups made to the exact design I'd dreamed of.

My grandson, Ben, the man's great-grandson, fished with those tipups the other day. And I watched proudly as he landed northern pike on them.

There's a time coming soon in the future when three grandsons will inherit those forty-year-old gifts. I'll divvy them up, and each will get his share.

And maybe a long way down the road, a son of their own just might ask where those old lines came from.

If that happens, there's a story they can tell; a tale of a long ago Christmas legacy from a kind and gentle man.

"Sheldon Wight"

Bingo's Place

Up in the wilds of Ontario, there's a little three-room cabin tucked against the base of a tree-speckled ridge of gray bedrock granite. At its front, the waters of Whitefish Lake reach almost to the doorstep of the pint-sized palace plunked in the popples and pines.

I call it "Bingo's place," named for Melvin "Bingo" Lange, a retired game warden and expert outdoorsman from Rhinelander. And there, at the tail end of March, six of us holed up for the better part of a week, to do battle with the fish of Whitefish.

Actually the place is part of Johnny Lark's fishing camp. But Bingo Lange has been coming there for so long that Lark just routinely sets the joint aside for Bingo's use two weeks each year, one in December, the other in March. Thus, the cabin's come to be known as "Bingo's place".

There Lange holds court with buddies, such as we, to lead the assault against mighty perch and walleyes.

Spend a few days there with Lange, and you come away with memories that dreams are made of. Employing a wry, dry sense of humor honed by his many years of working in the world of a warden, good old Bingo keeps the joint jumping. Yet beneath all the fun and games, lies the firmness of an iron hand; one that's camouflaged within a velvet glove.

Bingo, you see, is good at communication, both verbal and non-verbal. And he always makes his point.

Like he told the waitress in the restaurant, crowded with snappy-dressed people out for Sunday morning breakfasts, in Superior on the way up. The six of us, plus five more destined to reside in the cabin next door to Bingo's place, eleven in all, were gathered around a long table, dressed in our fishing trip wool shirts and blue jeans.

Hungry, we all ordered big breakfasts of eggs and pancakes and sausage, a meal capable of satisfying the best of appetites. After we'd scarfed the goodies down, the waitress arrived with our checks.

Old Bing gave her his best serious look and said, "Something in this food spoiled my appetite!" Well, the poor girl almost fainted and started to apologize. P t then she caught on, and joined in on the laughter th ocked the room.

Let's take the non-verbal. Bing is a wizard when it comes to body language.

Let's say you trot in a little mud on your boots up at his cabin. Bingo won't say a word — the first time. Out he'll come with his squeegee mop to solemnly repair the damage to his linoleum. And the offender quickly gets the message.

And let the garbage can begin to overflow. Slowly, silently Bing will tie a twistee to the black plastic bag, and set the lumpy heap in the middle of the kitchen. Up jumps a volunteer to haul the Hefty out the door.

Ask what's for supper? Bing will settle a trifle deeper into his easy chair, draw deep on his cigar, and blow a blue cloud of smoke across the room. He'll pause, not say a word. The smoke answers the question. Slowly it seems to shape into script that says, "Fix it! It's your turn to cook!"

Oh, there are times when he can be less subtle, more direct. Like the discussion over sleeping quarters at the breakfast table in Superior. "When you go in the cabin, the bedroom on the left, the lower bunk; that's mine!" he announced. Nobody misunderstood!

I watched the guy in action out on the ice. The first morning, before daylight, I pulled up behind his pickup. There he stood in my headlights, his ice auger already in hand. In the stillness, he hollered, "Becker, you got a set of jumper cables? My power auger won't start! The battery's dead!"

To readers uninitiated to ice fishing, power augers don't have batteries and you can't jump start 'em. But leave it to Bingo to inject a good laugh into a cold Canadian dawn.

Let the fishing drag, and he'll find a way to spice up sagging spirits. Like his line to Larry Keith that I heard floating across the ice. "Hey, Larry! I borrowed your coffee cup. But it's clean! I washed it in the minnow pail."

One day after lunch, the guy says to me, "Let's take a ride. Maybe we'll see some wildlife." So four of us, in two pickups, head down the narrow road through the Canadian bush.

Suddenly, he hits the brakes, and he and his partner, Al Spindler, pile out, looking into the woods. "There's a moose!" they almost whisper to Fran Barton and me. And there back in the popples and balsams stood a moose, black, big as a horse. The only moose I've seen in my life! A thrill I'll never forget. A fitting climax to a great fishing trip.

Thanks, Bingo! Thanks VERY much.

A God-Given Fish

I'm stiff! I'm sore! I hurt! My neck won't turn, and I think I stripped a gear in my right shoulder. Three days of heavy fishing is rough on an old codger.

Hang a compass bearing northeast, follow it for a couple hundred miles, and you'll be in the neighborhood of L'Anse, Michigan; a town snuggled between a blanket of vast maple and birch forests and the sheets of the crystal clear waters of Keweenaw Bay, an arm of Lake Superior.

L'Anse — where a long, downhill street branches off U.S. 41 to deadend at a boat landing; a community dashed with quaintness and charm, sprinkled with old-time peak-roofed bungalows and a beautiful ancient brownstone Catholic church, the steeple of which etches the skyline; and modern-day ranch homes, set in the shadows of tall spruces, to command spectacular views of the pristine lake.

Stand in L'Anse, and one gets the feeling that a ton of woes have been shed back up the road a piece.

The trip had been planned for months. Last November a bunch of us older-type cronies had gathered for a final fishing fling. "Next spring, when the ice goes out at L'Anse, we've got to go up there," Dick Birkholz, a high guru in our fishing fraternity, had said. "That's when the trout and salmon come in."

"Bob Becker holds his nine-pound Rainbow Trout from Lake Superior"

And so it came to pass. Four of us; Birkholz, myself; Johnny Walker, a former keeper of the prestigious Hertel Hall of Fishing Fame in the back room of his grocery store there; and Bill Barton, a retired game warden, and now an ordinary guy like the rest of us.

Two boats we'd brought; and as we dropped them into the cold water, a stiff southwest breeze whitecapped the bay. Hug the shore, I decided as I eased the boat upwind. I'm a respecter of the big lake. I have no desire to be a candidate for the Coast Guard.

Cutting the motor out from the big Celotex ceiling tile plant, Walker and I began our fishing. We'd drift downwind and cast, throwing small heavy spoons; Little Cleos in silver, blue, orange and lime green.

Maybe 200 yards and wham! "There's a fish!" I hollered to Walker up in the bow, my light spinning rod bent almost double. The fish hung deep, making powerful runs that screeched the brake of my little reel. Five minutes, and the fish gave us a look at it.

"A rainbow!" Walker announced. "A nice one." Another five and the trout was in the net — 25 inches, six pounds on Walker's scale. "Johnny," I said, "That was worth the price of admission!"

"Look's like Dick's got one on too," John said, eyeing the other boat. And in time, the net came out and a five pound king salmon was landed. We were off to a great start. And when day turned to dark, three cohos and a second king had been added to our bag.

Dawn broke like a dream the next morning; soft, grey, and warm. As my boat coasted to a stop, overhead flocks of geese honked on their northward journey. Goldeneyes and mergansers whistled by. But more important, were the fish that were dimpling the surface.

In short order, Walker and I tied three cohos in the three pound class, the other boat two.

Slowly, eastward, before a gentle morning breeze we drifted. Methodically, mechanically, I cast my orange Cleo, retrieving fast enough only to give the lure a life-like wobble in the water.

The fish hit at the end of the cast, way out, so solid that for a moment I thought I was snagged. Down deep it stayed, giving no quarter as I put all the pressure I dared on the eight-pound line.

Five minutes, ten, and my rod arm was aching. Finally, a roll on the surface. A humongous rainbow! Its iridescent violet-hued stripe flashing. Gradually, carefully, I pumped the spectacular trout toward the boat. And each time, on seeing us, away it would go, ripping a hundred feet of line from my screaming reel.

Could I land it, I wondered. With a feather touch, I worked the trout. And at last, fifteen minutes after I'd hooked it by Walker's time, he slipped his big net under the magnificent fish. Nine pounds, just under 28 inches long, it measured.

"Johnny," I said, "I've fished for over fifty years. But that's gotta be one of the high points."

And it was. For me, that rainbow was a God-given fish; one the kind of which only the fondest of fishing dreams and memories are made.

Charlie Cool

Three fishermen in a boat — three generations; a grandfather, his son and a grandson.

My two grandsons came over for a visit a Sunday or two
ago. Kyle and Jesse's their names. But I've nicknamed them
Charlie and Mighty Cool. They're going on four and two.

Mighty's still too small to appreciate fishing. He's more
interested in pounding with his little plastic toy hammer and
pushing Momma's antique doll buggy, the one she had as a
little girl, down the hall.

But Charlie, that's a different story. He's into everything,
including fishing. "I'm big now, aren't I," he tells the world.

Late last March, at the tail end of the ice fishing, he'd
been promised a fishing outing. But it'd rained all that day.
"He'd be a big blotter out there on the ice," I told his mom
and dad. And so, disappointed, he had to stay home with
Grandma. "You be a good boy," I bribed him, "and I'll take
you fishing in my big boat when summer comes."

And his day came this recent Sunday. First, a trip to the
basement to scoop a dozen nightcrawlers from my washtub
worm farms; a fun thing. Little boys and big worms go well
together.

Then, wearing the dandy many-colored fishing cap his
mom had bought him, sitting proud between me and his dad,

we headed for a little lake loaded with hungry bluegills, a fish created with kids in mind. There, at the boat landing, his dad strapped him into his fancy yellow life preserver.

As I eased the boat away from the landing with the oars, I could see he was nervous, his hands tightly gripping the boat seat. And I understood his fears. "Should I go slow with the motor?" I asked. "Yeah," came back his hushed one-word answer.

I rigged his little bamboo pole, set a tiny yellow bobber, and began to impale a worm on his hook. By then, Charlie was over being scared, back to his own cool self, watching my every move. "Why do fish eat worms?" he asked. "They taste good," I told him.

"Why-y-y?" came his reply. And I couldn't give him a good answer.

I flipped out his line and propped up his pole. Charlie, you see, was too busy poking in the minnow pail, watching the gentle waves splash against the side of the boat; to hold it. "Watch your bobber, Kyle," his dad said to him. "I think you got a bite. Pull him up!"

And from the depths came a six-inch bluegill, one that had to be placed in a pail of water "to take home to show mom."

The morning moved along, Charlie catching bluegills, missing many amongst his fidgeting. And as noon approached, his dad diplomatically announced to him, "We're going to have to leave soon. This afternoon we're going to take Mom fishing. And you get to stay home and play with Grandma."

Well, the psychology almost worked. It threw Charlie for a minute or two. Silently he sat meditating. But then, turning to his dad and, in his best con-man manner, said, "You know dad, when a grandpa and a dad and a mom go fishing — they're supposed to take a little boy along!"

Talk about little wheels turning! The kid showed me something there!

But, what with the fresh air and a good lunch in his tum-tum, by afternoon his eyelids were drooping, and he willingly adjourned for a nap. Grandma settled into her rocking chair to watch the Cubs; and Dad, Mom and I sneaked off for some serious fishing.

The walleyes cooperated, and when darkness fell, we headed home. There at the door, in his jammies, Charlie met us, flashing his best dimpled smile, glad to see his mom and dad once more.

And as Dad and I worked filleting our catch, back and forth he moved between us, inspecting our work. "That's a nice job you're doing there, Dad!" I heard him tell his father.

Then over to me to stand on a chair. "Where's the guts?" he said matter-of-factly. "I want to see the guts!"

"There they are," I answered, poking with my knife. "Oh!" he replied.

Finally, the day's work was done, and the crew began to pack for home. Charlie was beginning to wind down, to drag a bit.

Yet, I was hoping he'd have enough energy left to again tell his grandma what he'd said on an earlier visit, a conversation as he sat eating a dish of chocolate ice cream with her.

"Grandma," he'd said then, "I'm going to be nice to you. I'm going to leave grandpa here with you. I won't take him home with me!"

I liked that. That Charlie's a cool kid.

In Memory of Geoff Emerson

No man is an island, it's been said, a truism with which I essentially agree.

But I also know that a man's spirit can live on an island. I know, because I saw it come to pass the other day.

First, the island. And then the man.

It's a majestic island – stuck in a far corner of the Chippewa Flowage. I'm not going to say exactly where it is. Because if I did, that would only detract from its solemn sanctity. Better that people discover its secret on their own, in the course of their fishing and camping visits to its shores.

The island today, remains pretty much the way the good Lord created it. Rising abruptly from the pristine waters of the Flowage, its rocky, sandy soils support a dense stand of virgin white pines, trees that tower a hundred feet in the air, some three feet thick at their bases. And in their needled crowns, the winds sigh softly.

Overhead eagles soar, riding the breezes on motionless wings, as they have for thousands of years. Off its banks, loons swim and dive, piercing the dusk of peaceful summer evenings with their eerie calls.

Owned by the state, which is all of us, the island's only a couple acres; a mini-wilderness, lost, yet surviving in a world rapidly passing it by. But, in that lonely obscurity lies

"Geoff Emerson"

its unique sacredness. For now it holds to its breast some of the soul of a man, one who loved wild things — like the island so aptly typifies.

His name was Geoff Emerson. He died last October of cancer. Only forty, he was struck down at the pinnacle of his life, leaving a wife and two young sons.

And on a recent cool, sun-filled, northwoods afternoon, a hundred of us gathered on the little remote patch of earth to memorialize him, to commit to posterity a bit of what he believed in, and stood for.

Emerson, at his death, was a Department of Natural Resources employee, the assistant director of DNR's Northwest District. He was responsible for far-reaching, complex activities like wildlife and fish management, law enforcement, state parks and forests, programs that are the very foundation of our life style here.

But let no one be led to believe that the man was recognized because of his performance of those bureaucratic duties. Far be it. Emerson was commemorated for contributions that never showed on his paycheck.

"He had a special quality about him, like the Chippewa Flowage," John Plenke, DNR's chief conservation warden for the district, told me. "He loved the wilderness, eagles, the call of the loon."

And so, the hundred of us, friends and relatives from places like Minnesota, Ohio, Indiana, Madison, Racine and Wisconsin Rapids, came to the island. There, on a south-facing slope where it catches the sun, at the base of a tall pine, we dedicated a bronze plaque to the man.

"Enjoy this island....it is dedicated to the memory of GEOFF EMERSON — for his belief in the miracle of creation....and his spirit of fun" it reads.

Two words — "creation" and "fun"! They exemplify the man.

A fisheries biologist by background, Emerson was a graduate of Purdue University. "He believed in science," his father told us. "But he also believed in God!"

A co-worker spoke of Emerson's fight with cancer. "When he was under treatment, he told me once, 'worrying is for atheists,'" she said.

A fishing buddy told of sitting in a boat with Geoff on a northern Wisconsin lake. "He paused, looking at the beauty surrounding us, and said 'every kid from Chicago should spend a day up here!'"

Another talked of Emerson's initial contacts with the Northern States Power Company that led to the state's purchase of the company's lands on the Flowage, including the very island we were standing on.

And after the speech-making was over, I visited with Barb Emerson, Geoff's widow. "How do your boys feel about this?" I asked.

"They like it very much," she answered. "They're already calling it 'dad's island.'"

Dad's Island — a good name if I ever heard one.

Bone Lake Muskie Tales

To catch a muskie! Ah, yes! That can be a challenge.

"You don't fish for muskies," my fishing chum, Joe Zanter, said matter-of-factly from the back of the boat, as he heaved a yellow bucktail across the water. "You hunt for muskies."

And how right he was. No portion of the fishing fraternity places more value on the amenities of fishing, versus hanging finny critters on a stringer, than does the muskie fishing clan.

Three of us; Zanter, myself, and Bill Barton, were on Bone Lake over near Luck. The lake is renowned as one of Wisconsin's top muskie waters. Over time, Bone has been very kind to me. Years back, when my fishing blood flowed considerably hotter; I, or people in my boat, once caught seven legal muskies on seven consecutive trips to Bone; a record that I've never come close to equaling on any other lake.

I've fished with Zanter and Barton many times. The trips always start the same, enthusiasm and anticipation firing us up; whether we're chasing walleyes, northerns, perch or trout. But when we're after muskies, the mood's a bit more subdued. We know the odds are stacked against us; that we're playing poker with a marked deck, and the muskie's the dealer.

So there's an air of joviality. What the heck, go fishing and have some fun, some good laughs. Don't take it too seriously! Work hard at it, to be sure. But when the day's done; well, measure its success in psychic rewards, not numbers of fish caught.

"I've had good luck along this shore," I told the two, as Zanter set his boat on a drift a cast-length out from an underwater weed edge. The late-July day seemed perfect, overcast, on the muggy side, a steady southerly breeze pushing us before it.

For an hour, we pounded the gray water with casts. "Time for a sandwich," Barton volunteered as noon approached.

"Not me," I replied. "No eating til I see a fish." And a couple of good hearty snorts from him and Zanter. "You might just starve to death!" they needled, as they dove into their nosebags.

"OK! OK!" I came back. "But up ahead where that pontoon boat's parked, there's a bar that breaks out into the lake. I can always raise a fish there."

Now, bragging has no place in muskie fishing. It's risky, the mark of the inexperienced. Yet, their barbs had bruised my angling ego. And I worked my black bucktail a bit more seriously as the secret spot approached. And I called my shot.

"There's one!" I hollered, as a three-foot muskie, nose-tight to my lure, came into view, swirling at the boat, only to disappear. "NOW I can eat."

Through the day we fished, the hours spiced with periodic "lookers," muskies that follow baits but won't strike. And a steady stream of well-warped outdoor tales.

Like Barton boasting about the retriever dog he once

owned.

Seems like Bill was out duck hunting one Fall and shot a nice mallard. "Fetch!" he ordered faithful old Fido. Into the lake, Fido leaped to make the retrieve. Swimming to where the duck had disappeared; the dog dove underwater, and came back with a northern pike in its mouth.

"And do you know, inside that northern was my duck!" Barton said. And with a straight face!

Well, one lie can't stand alone. So Zanter's turn.

"This guy had a pointer one time," he told. "He was out hunting pheasants, and the dog disappeared. Well, he looked and looked, but couldn't find the dog. Well, the next spring he was wandering through the area. And there, he came upon the skeleton of a dog, upright with one front foot poised in the air!"

"And you'll never believe this, but there in front of its nose, was the skeleton of a pheasant!"

And that's the way the day went, folks. You guessed it. We never caught a muskie.

Oh! I did forget one thing. Zanter ran out of gas a mile from the boat landing, and he had to limp in on his electric trolling motor.

And that's no lie.

Serves him right for telling such outrageous untruths.

Goodbye Summer

The pots and pans were scrubbed, the campsite policed. Packsacks and coolers are again loaded. And one by one, the boats head into the cloud-dappled sunset, the sounds of their outboards fading into the dusk's gentle quiet, the waves from their wakes gently sliding across the lake's grey face.

Raindrops, from an anemic shower overhead, dimple the water around me. I reach for the starter rope, give it a tug. The Mercury springs to life, and I ease the boat away from the lonely island.

At low throttle, ever so slowly, purposely, I slip back from its wooded shore. Skimming the pine and maple tops, an osprey coasts by. Blue smoke, the last remnants of our campfire, hangs in a mist-like haze in the green foliage.

A last look at the scene, I want; a bit of nostalgic memory to carry away with me, something to fuel me through the winter ahead.

Summer's over. The shorelunch had signalled its end. And I'm saying my farewell.

We've got this little fishing club, you see; a group of guys who, as the letterhead on its stationary reads, are dedicated to good sportsmanship. For twenty years now, we've been gathering once a month, to fish for muskies.

Not that we catch that many. We don't. A dozen fish a

summer over the legal size is a good year. And it's been a long time since I've seen one put on a stringer, even Mike Johnson's 46-incher last year. It went back into the lake, not on the wall.

Yet, we're serious. The guys work hard at it. But there's more to fishing than just the catching. And that's where the club puts its priorities. Call it socializing; call it good fellowship; call it friendship. For that, more than anything else, is what draws us together.

And our summer shorelunches are the heart of that kinship. For it's at those, that the real rewards, the true purpose of the clan, has its being.

Come late in the afternoon, we gather. In singles and pairs, the boats filter in, tieing to birch trees and alder bushes on islands that the state owns here in our northern lakes. Handshakes and greetings are exchanged. Few of us make all of the outings. Many only one. Old bonds must be renewed.

And the tales of the day's adventures begin to flow. Like Bill Barton's wail of woe about the big one that had smacked his yellow Globe surface lure, right beside his boat, ripping the reel handles from his hand. "Look at this!" Bill says, proudly waving a bloody thumb, a patch of skin gone from it.

Tony Jelich's over from Solon Springs. Metro Maznio down from Cable, and we rap about trout fishing.

Len Urquhart, who's pushing eighty-something, is there fishing with Len Hoefferle. They know their muskie fishing. "I put him into a good fish," Urquhart says, pointing to Hoefferle. "But he lost it. A nut fell off his reel!"

Today, John Plenke's the bull cook. "The chowder's ready, you guys!" he hollers. And the line begins to form.

Charlie Tollander's at its head. He takes one look and says, "Umm! This is a feast fit for a king!"

Plenke and his helper, John Parker, have done a superb job. Stacked high on the weather-beaten, lop-sided old picnic table is a spread rarely seen in the wilds.

A pile of yellow sweetcorn rests steaming, and eager hands dive into it. Two big northern pike and a nice rainbow trout, baked to perfection, repose in a long pan. A stainless-steel bowl of tossed salad, a cast-iron pot of baked beans, hot from the fire. A tray of wild-rice-spiced stuffing. Zucchini squash topped with tomatos and a couple kinds of exotic cheeses, bubbles in a black skillet. Warmed golden garlic bread. And a big pot of coffee to wash it all down.

The conversation shifts. There's still fishing talk, but more about the food. "Good job, John!" they tell Plenke. "There's plenty here!" he responds. And most of the 24 of us on hand go back for seconds.

But in time, bellies are stroked, and red bandannas come out to wipe butter streaks from chins, and fish crumbs from mustaches. The party's winding down. In pairs, the fishermen board their boats. A wave of hands, 'see ya's,' and they're on their way.

Another shorelunch is over. Another muskie fishing trip is history.

"Goodbye, summer," I whisper.

And I gun the throttle.

"An unidentified fisherwomen and her twenty-pound Chinook Salmon"

Lordy, How She Could Fish!

She was a pretty young lady — tall, willowy, about twenty-five I'd say. And she was a sight to see, what with her long blond hair flowing in the wind, standing thigh-deep in the cold waters of Lake Michigan, dressed in chest-high khaki-brown waders.

For three days I watched the lady as she fished. And believe me, she was good at it.

Now, over the last fifty years or so, I've been around a ton of fishermen, males that is. I've come to recognize the good from the poor. It doesn't take much to tell the difference. Look for the way they handle a rod, how they net a hooked fish.

But this young lady; well, she knew the business. That became obvious, as I watched her across the hundred yards of water that separated our fishing party from hers.

Five of us had met at Marinette recently, to try our hand at some salmon fishing. This time of the year the big chinooks, or "kings" as they're called, pull in to the shore to spawn. And they produce a spectacular brand of fishing action.

Good ol' Lake Michigan and I are not exactly strangers. I was born and raised within sight of her shores. As a teenager I spend a lot of hours around her long piers and rock-filled breakwaters with a fish pole. And, as I caught perch and ciscos, I'd watch the fishing tugs chug out of the harbor on their way to tend their lake trout nets.

But then the St. Lawrence River Seaway was built, opening the Great Lakes to ocean-going ships. And through the seaway swam a critter called the sea lamprey, an eel-like predator that attacked the lake trout, all but destroying the lake's population.

Thus began a thirty-year chapter of rehabilitation work, lamprey control and restocking. The results are well-known. The work not only brought the lake trout back, but the introduction of new species, coho and chinook salmon, produced fishing opportunities and success beyond the wildest dreams.

And that's why we'd come to Marinette.

Friends over in the eastern part of the state had issued the invitation. "Come on over," they'd said, "and we'll try for some chinooks. They run big, up to twenty pounds."

It's a different kind of fishing, monotonous in some respects, because the big fish have honeymooning on their minds and are not voracious feeders. So it's cast, cast, cast; throwing heavy metal lures of various colors across the water.

But every so often, one of those big hummers decides to take a whack at a bait, and it's almost heart-attack city. Fast and powerful, the big fish can strip off a hundred yards of line in nothing flat, causing reel drags to scream. Into the air, four to five feet, they'll leap; falling back into the water with explosion-like splashes.

We fished from boats, but others waded the shorelines — like the young lady's party of six. They knew the ropes, outfishing us several times over, as they cast their orange and silver spoons. All caught fish. Yet, she was the star.

For there she stood at six-o'clock in the morning when we arrived to launch our boats. And there she stood, in the dark of evening as we departed.

Let me tell you, she put on a show; expertly, smoothly, whipping out baits in long casts, nonchalantly chatting with her companions. And when one of her friends was into a fish, she'd pick up the big, long-handled net, wade out into exactly the right position; and with a deft, darting motion, the huge writhing salmon would be in the net.

Have her hook a fish herself, and she played the fish with skills that were a joy to witness. Rod tip up, adjusting the reel's drag, keeping the pressure on.

"Look at that!" Tom Kullman remarked, as I eased my boat into the landing for the trip home. "She's got another one on!"

I turned, and sure enough, there the young lady stood in the mid-morning sunshine; smiling, laughing, her rod bowed as she fought a wildly thrashing big chinook.

Lordy, how that lady could fish!

"Dick Birkholz toasts a sandwich on Upper Michigan's Perch Lake"

Let Me Count The Ways

How should a fishing trip be measured?

The question rolled through my mind as I headed the pickup home; toward Wisconsin. By the number of fish caught? By the companionship? By a special experience? And my pondering reminded me of the romantic words of an ancient poet — "How much do I love thee? Let me count the ways!"

There we were; three of us, Dick Birkholz, Johnny Walker and I; winding down a December ice fishing junket to Michigan's upper peninsula. Combine our ages, and the total would push nearly 200 years. And it's a safe bet that a goodly portion of that time has been spent with a fish pole in our hands.

Yet, frozen stiff behind me in the box of the truck rested only four measly walleyes, not much to show for our efforts.

We'd gone back — back to waters we'd fished last summer, a lake that had been ever so kind to us then, where stringers had hung heavy with fish alongside the boat. And perhaps that had been a mistake. Sometimes it's better, you see, to not go back; to leave good fishing memories lie undisturbed, untarnished by the fickleness of the gods that rule on fishing trips.

And so I was rationalizing as I drove, looking for the good

things we'd known the three previous days. I had no trouble finding them.

For example, there was Sidnaw, Michigan; a slumbering, peaceful bit of humanity impaled like a shishkebab on State Highway 28. I love Sidnaw. If you ever decide to escape from it all, I recommend the place.

"What's the population of Sidnaw?" I asked Tom Thompson, owner of the local minimart gas station, purveyor of fishing lore, and renter of cabins. "Oh, about a hundred. Mostly retired folks, like you," he came back.

And there in one of Thompson's comfy, cozy cabins, we set up our base camp — just off the end of the runway of the little airstrip, which we promptly dubbed "Sidnaw International."

Twelve miles south, through the wild desolately beautiful Ottawa National Forest, lies Perch Lake; the object of our fishing attention. Each morning, at daybreak, I drove the twisting trail through the dense woods.

And I enjoyed every minute of it.

Past long-abandoned farmfields where old cedar fence posts lean, and rusty barbed wires sag, telling their tale of another era when strong-willed pioneers tried, and failed, to carve livelihoods from the thin soil. Past the myriads of balsams and spruces, their branches flocked with snow, seeding in on the old pastures; Mother Nature's way of saying "I am the boss!"

Ahead a hundred yards, a little buck prances across the road; to pause, staring at us from a thicket of popples a hundred feet off the road. And the face of a brilliant sunrise, orange and red and pink against the eastern shoreline of the lake. The slow morning drives were sheer pleasure.

We fished hard, drilling more holes in Perch's ice and

covering more of its acres than I care to remember, doggedly trying to unlock the secrets of its walleyes and big perch. Michigan allows two winter fishing lines. So we each set out a tipup and fished a second jigging pole. All the old tried-and-true lures and techniques were tested — Swedish pimples tipped with waxies and minnows, Rapalas of different sizes and colors.

And the bottom line was that nothing produced. A handful of walleyes, no perch, no crappies, no bluegills. Which is really weird because last summer, we caught fine panfish.

Yet as I headed home, my creel held a limit of good memories.

Like the immense, almost overpowering silence that encompasses the Michigan wilderness this time of the year. Like the carpet of fresh snow that sparkled like billions of diamonds in the morning sunshine, and the cheery noon campfire on the shore to toast our sandwiches and warm our spirits. Like the big, bushy-tailed, black timber wolf that padded slowly across the ice to look us over, to see what or who was invading his domain.

Like the recollections of suppers rustled by a cook waddling around in longjohns. Like spicy bratwursts peeking from a bowl of steaming sauerkraut to soothe the appetite after a cold hard day on the ice.

They're the real and true measurements of a fishing trip, I decide.

Like let me count the ways.

Their Own Worst Enemy

"Blip!" The little yellow styrofoam bobber pops beneath the surface of the water of my fishing hole, pausing there, the trademark of a big bluegill biting. I set the hook, and the flimsy fiberglass jigging pole dips and dances, the two-pound test monofilament line squeaking in its guides. And to the top of the ice, I nurse a floppy eight-inch bluegill, brilliant in its hues of blue-black, green and orange.

Is bluegill fishing improving around the area? I'd like to think so. This winter I saw some nice catches of gills, and heard a number of reports of others.

And that's good to see. Because the bluegill, to my way of thinking, provides more sport, all-year long, than any other species of fish. The bluegill is to fishing what the cottontail rabbit is to hunting, and the popple tree is to logging.

No other fish is pursued more diligently by anglers, winter and summer. Without a doubt, I'd say the bluegill is the first fish that the vast majority of our youngsters catch. Toss a worm-baited hook and a bobber off the dock of almost any lake in Wisconsin, and the odds are good that a bluegill will be waiting to grab it.

True, the gills may be only three or four inches long, what fishermen sometimes call "watch fobs." But they'll be there, and in numbers.

And therein lies the bluegill's biggest problem. The bluegill is its own worst enemy! For it's the tremendous reproductive capacity of the species that often limits its ability to reach decent size. "Stunting" it's called — too many fish for the available food supply. The result is a high population of fish, but very few considered keepable by fishermen.

To find out what's going on to improve bluegill fishing, I visited the other day with Howard Snow, a DNR fish research biologist stationed at Spooner. Snow has been conducting research projects on bluegills since 1957.

"Northwest Wisconsin is one of the best areas in the state for bluegills," Snow told me. "However, the rates of growth can vary considerably from lake to lake."

I asked Snow to describe the characteristics of a productive bluegill lake.

"A number of factors enter the picture," he said. "Fertility is a big one. The more dissolved solids; nutrients, algae, plankton — the better the growth. Water depth also plays a part. Shallow lakes that have a history of partial winter freeze-out usually produce good bluegill growth. But the biggest factor is the density of the bluegill population itself."

For the past several years, Snow has been sampling bluegill populations in 115 lakes in northwest Wisconsin. He's discovered some interesting things.

A key finding has been the fact that slow-growing bluegills usually are not found in lakes where walleyes are a major predator. His conclusions suggest that walleyes may be more effective than northern pike or largemouth bass in controlling slow-growing panfish. Snow speculates that the night feeding habits of the walleye are the reason.

So on three lakes; Anderson in Barron County, Little

"Winter Bluegill fishing is great sport"

Mirror in Polk, and Clear in Sawyer, Snow has stocked year-old walleyes of 7 to 8 inches in length to feed on the stunted bluegills present.

"First we go in with nets and remove up to fifty percent of the intermediate size (2-6 inch) bluegills," he explained. "The purpose is to get the population down to where the walleyes can have an effect on it."

Snow calls the procedure 'biomanipulation'. "What we're doing is artificially disturbing the population," he said. "On Anderson Lake, we got some good results, increased growth and larger fish."

Snow talked about the time it takes to grow a 'good' bluegill. "On the average an eight inch fish will be 8 to 9 years old in this area," he noted.

And what effect does angling pressure have on bluegill populations? Snow feels that it doesn't have much impact, except on a few lakes where fishing pressure is unusually heavy.

That's good news. We're fortunate indeed to have such an abundant bluegill fishery in this area. The gill has often been referred to as the gamest of all fishes for its size. Ask anyone who fishes for gills with a light fly rod in the summer. They'll more than agree.

Then fillet the little beauties, coat 'em with a batter, pop 'em into a deep fryer — and there's nothing finer on the table either!

Bait Shops

Fishing season's coming on, and my thoughts turn to bait shops.

Bait shops — bless 'em — are one of the last vestiges of small-town northern Wisconsinana. Perhaps nothing perpetuates the nostalgia of our north better than an old-fashioned bait shop. Fifty years ago, every little crossroads hamlet had one or two. Today many remain, relatively untouched by the passage of time.

Years back, I'd come north, on fishing trips with my Uncle Herb; and into a bait shop we'd walk for a supply of mud minnows...finny critters to chase the walleyes with. Inside the door I'd enter a wondrous world; dark, dank and damp, perfumed with fishy scent that titillated my young nose, nostrils eager to get about the business of catching fish.

Rising from a creaky, time-worn, swivel chair; wearing a battered red-and-black wool shirt and a floppy, sweat-stained felt hat; sporting the stubble of a three-day beard; the proprietor would extend a gnarled right hand the size of a small ham.

"Well, hello there Herb!" he'd announce. "Good to see you again. Up for some fishing, I see."

"That we are, Hank!" Unk would answer. "How they biting?"

And so the conversation would go, talk of walleyes and northerns and lakes where big ones had been caught.

All the while, I'd wander; feasting my eyes on the black masses of fatheads and chubs swimming in their concrete tanks, eyeing the ranks of Daredevils and Heddon River Runts resting under the glass counter top, scratched and lined by years of quarters and half-dollars, of an ancient oaken showcase.

Look and you can still find these bastions of my boyhood. True, our modern age is catching up to them. There's competition, for example, from the super-service stations; spic and span, with their neon signs out front and nice young ladies tending computerized cash registers, enterprises that handle everything from gas to groceries.

But they're really not bait shops. Bait shops are elite, exclusive establishments. Places that project an aristocratic aura, spiced with the smells of shiners and nightcrawlers, replete with old calendars hanging from their walls, and manned by friendly talkative folks content in what they're doing.

Over the years, I've found bait shop operators to be fountains of fishing knowledge. A stop for a couple dozen fatheads need only take five minutes. But the talk about what's going on in the outdoors can take a half-hour or more.

No better advice could I give a visiting fisherman than to spend a few extra minutes shooting the breeze with the guy who sells the bait. A lot of good information can be gained.

And some home-spun humor too.

Like the deeply philosophical discussion I once got into with an operator in Cumberland over the nature of truth. No fisherman, he contended, ever tells the truth; a position with which I firmly disagreed; arguing instead, that some do — but noone believes them.

And the tale about the fisherman that came in for a supply of minnows. After filling the order, the operator casually blessed the pail with the sign of the cross.

Well, the man apparently had good fishing success. Because the next day he was back for a refill, telling the operator, in all seriousness, "And be sure you bless them again!"

Duncan Hanacek, who runs one of my local bait shops in Spooner, tells of a lady who came in for minnows. In her hand, she carried only the inner strainer of a minnow pail, a container incapable of holding water!

"She was pretty embarrassed," Duncan said. "But I solved the problem by putting a plastic bag inside and sent her happily on her way."

Bait shops are businesses, to be sure. But they're a lot more. Like the old-time country store, they're places where human relations are still practiced at their finest, where people are still greeted and treated with warmth and respect.

The next time you're in one, look around. You might just find me back by the fathead tank.

God's Little Acre II

I call the place "God's Little Acre II"...a takeoff on the classic novel by Erskine Caldwell many years ago, a book about life in the Old South.

Only my 'little acre' is here in the North, a tiny plot of ground in a campground on a wild, remote lake deep inside the Ottawa National Forest in Michigan's upper peninsula.

And there; three of us, Johnny Walker, Dick Birkholz and I, spent some time recently, camping and fishing.

It's a beautiful little parcel. Resting on a knoll overlooking the pristine blue waters of Perch Lake, snuggled in the arms of tall maples and stately hemlocks. Campsite 15, it's officially called by the U.S. Forest Service, the people that run the place.

There you can pitch your tent, roll out your sleeping bag, build a campfire; and morning, noon, and night renew your ties with Mother Earth, and recharge the batteries of life.

Like the mornings, for instance. Ten minutes to five, my pocket watch says, as I upzip the door fly of the tent and step outside. Except for the soft call of a bird from the surrounding woods, all is still. Just over the eastern horizon, a peeking sun is doing its best to burn off the cloak of white bridal-veil-like mist that clothes the lake; eerily shrouding a pine-covered island, like a scene from an old Alfred Hitchcock

*"Upper Michigan's Perch Lake produced a fine catch for
Dick Birkholz and John Walker"*

movie.

It's a scene well-worth getting up for, and I drink it in.

And the noons, the middays when we come in for our sandwiches and siestas. That's when the little acre is mottled with sunshine and shade. Dragonflies dart erratically, and chipmunks come for the peanuts I lay out on our firewood. A black mallard duck, accustomed to people, waddles up from the water's edge to beg for morsels of bread.

And the nights! Ah, yes, they're the best of all. It's then that we gather, tired after a long day's fishing, in shadowy dusks to watch clouds of mayflies swirl against the sky. It's then that the campfire's built, the little charcoal grill fired up. It's then that Johnny Walker drops fresh-caught walleye fillets into a sizzling skillet, that he broils the venison bratwursts made from a buck he shot last fall.

And when the appetites have been staved once more, in a circle around the fire we huddle, resting, rehashing the day, sipping hot coffee from porcelain cups. Overhead, framed by the silhouettes of hemlock tops etched against the evening sky, the Big Dipper and the North Star hang. The fire snaps and crackles, its flickering flames sending sparks and smoke swirling upward to meld with the northern lights that flow, changing shapes and tones, chameleon-like, high above.

The drama is a rare one, a soul-depth experience that will stick in memories for a lifetime.

And the fishing? Each year, the three of us come to Perch, primarily for its walleyes. But also for its excellent panfish; perch, crappies, and bluegills.

This year the walleye fishing was good; not sensational, just good. We had to work for our fish for sure. We found them in a shallow bay so weed-choked that I've come to call it Walker's Swamp, so-termed because of Johnny's uncanny ability to entice walleyes to hit his rubber-minnow jigs there.

But all three of us caught walleyes. Birkholz prefers tiny jigheads tipped with a leech, and I the deer-hair jigs I tied last winter. Our technique was simple, let the boat drift downwind and work our lures through open pockets in the submerged vegetation.

It's a frustrating method of fishing in that the vast majority of the casts produce only a cluster of green water weeds on your hook. But if that's where the fish are, that's the price that has to be paid.

We'd hoped to get into the big jumbo perch that the lake holds, and tried hard for them. But not a single one did we catch. Perhaps the heavy hatches of mayflies that were taking place was the reason.

Yet, as said, it was fishing trip to remember. Three days of sights and sounds and good fellowship. Of eagles, ospreys, and wild geese; of sun-filled days and moon-filled nights; in air so pure and sweet that it should be bottled for posterity.

Such is life at God's Little Acre II!

The Lady Was Kind

The Beautiful Lady was in a good mood....that I could tell. I could hear her laughing long before I reached the ridgetop that marks the rim of the valley through which she flows. And it was music to my ears.

The Beautiful Lady, you see, is an old trout stream friend. She and I have been running around together for nigh onto twenty-five years now, a romance so intense, so special that words have yet to be contrived to describe it.

And I was on my way to visit her again, another of the dozen or so times I do each summer.

Barely seven o'clock, the morning world was just beginning to come to life. Overhead, dark clouds hung thickly, remnants of those that had dropped two inches of rain the previous day. My booted feet trod softly, not making a sound; the path I've walked so many times cushioned with spongy needles fallen from the white pines through which the little trail passes.

All is lush and green; the pines, the popples, the somber balsams, the ferns that clothe the forest floor with their delicate beauty. From the valley below, rises the sound of the Lady's laughter, greeting me. And through the verdant foliage, I catch the first glimpses of her, silver where the light strikes her, dark brown where she slides beneath overhanging trees.

"Few things in this world are more beautiful than a trout stream in the early morning," I tell myself. And I slip down the narrow trail to her side. There, where an old logging dam once stood, it's aged timbers still visible, the Lady pauses at the constriction, then rushes forward, sending her bankful charge of water crashing downstream over a bed of boulders in a crescendo of sound.

I step into the stream, feel the power of its current tugging against my legs, and begin my fishing. "If I don't catch a single fish today, this will still be fun!" I say to myself. And the stream and I become one.

Downstream first to fish a couple of deep holes, places where on similar occasions of high water, I've taken some fine brown trout, fish that seem to cast aside their usual skiddishness at such times.

The first pool yields only a small trout, released. I'm disappointed but not surprised. The hole is deteriorating, silting in badly. Where it once swirled too deep for my waders, now only a narrow thread through one side is worth fishing. For that's another thing about trout streams. They're constantly changing, never exactly the same from year to year.

And I move on, to my favorite stretch of stream, a run guarded by a giant spruce tree where the Lady flows wide and deep. Cautiously, like a heron stalking its prey, I move into position at the tail of the pool and begin my casting.

The rocky riffle at the head is hidden by the high water, yet I know exactly where it lies. And I drop my baited hook just at its base. Instantly the night crawler stops. I feel the tug of the trout as it mouths the bait, and set the hook. Around the pool the trout races, then finally splashing to my outstretched hand, a dandy pound-and-a-half brown.

On, upriver I move. As the day brightens, the trout become more active. A keeper brook trout joins the brown in the creel, and several small fish of both species are released.

Into an eddy of water swirling below a windfall, I cast. The crawler barely strikes the water's surface and a trout takes it. Another nice brown, chunky and hefty, it too is added to the bag.

Out of the Lady's steep-sided valley I wade and into the flat, marshy bottomland, where her waters meander lazily, and the marsh grass stands tall on her banks. Through the muck and mire I poke, flirting with slips and slides that bring the stream's water dangerously close to the top of my waders. Dragonflies dart. Marsh birds flit. And as the morning sun breaks through to shine on her face, the Lady smiles.

Along her way I pass, adding trout to my catch. A nice brookie, another fine brown.

And as I edge around the last bend, where I'll leave the Lady, the creel holds nine trout, one brook trout short of my limit. A good catch....I'm satisfied.

Yet there's room for a last cast or two. And from an overhanging bank, I take a final fish, a brookie that surely must have been destined for me.

Once again, the Lady'd been very kind.

Mississippi River White Bass

The sun rises red over the Mississippi River on late July mornings. Like a molten ball, it peeks slowly over the limestone bluffs marking the eastern bank of the river.

I know because I was there recently, there fishing.

But to catch fish from the Mississippi takes someone who knows the Mississippi. Someone who was born on it and knows its many moods and secrets. Someone like Elmer Sprick.

Elmer and I are long-time friends, going back to our forestry days with the old Wisconsin Conservation Department in the 50's. And Mavis, his wife, and Momma are too, back to times when our kids, now married with youngsters of their own, were in diapers.

Now retired, the Spricks reside at Lake City, Minnesota; a charming little river town that hugs the Mississippi's edge. There, built on a high bluff, their home overlooks Lake Pepin, a 30-mile long, 25,000 acre, three-mile-across widening of the big river.

There, at his country estate, Sprick grows a few Christmas trees, raises a big garden, entertains his many friends...and does a lot of fishing.

The invitation to visit had been long standing. So recently it came to pass. Bill and Evie Barton, also old friends of the Spricks, and Momma and I made the trip. The ladies would socialize and shop. The menfolks would fish.

The Mississippi is a majestic river; big, awesome, and steeped in history. Today, it's a corridor of commerce. Bordering its banks, railroads and highways bustle. On its waters, long barges pushed by towboats, carry loads of fuel northward to the Twin Cities, and grain southward to places like St. Louis and New Orleans. In marinas, scores of gleaming white sailboats stand moored, waiting for weekend recreationists.

But look closer and one can also savor the river's past. Civil War period homes and hotels, beautifully maintained, bring back visions of paddle-wheel steamboats; of Mark Twain and his offspring, Tom Sawyer and Huckleberry Finn.

"That's an old steamboat landing," Sprick commented, pointing from the rear seat of his boat to a spit of rocks jutting into the river.

The point marked a sandy bar that we were about to fish. The spot, Sprick said, was one of his favorites for walleyes, saugers, and white bass.

"Right now, the bass are our best chance," Sprick commented as we drifted downstream, casting our lures. "The walleyes are usually slow this time of year."

A half-hour's effort produced no action, and Sprick announced, "Let's go cruisin'!" And therein laid a new fishing dimension for me, that of looking for fish; white bass, feeding on the surface. Travelling in schools, the bass dimple the water as they drive shad minnows to the top.

In short order, with his binoculars, Sprick spotted a school in a weedy bay. And the fun began!

Casting white rubber-like lures called "Shad Tails" on large jig heads, we were quickly into the fish. The white bass

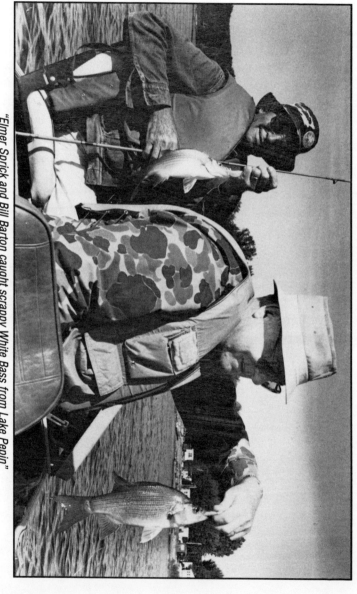

"Elmer Sprick and Bill Barton caught scrappy White Bass from Lake Pepin"

resemble crappies, but they fight more like smallmouth bass. At times the action was fast and furious. Double-headers, with two of us having fish on at the same time, were common. And a couple times, we had triple-headers, as all three of us battled fish.

The bass ranged up to fifteen inches and two pounds in size. And talk about fight! I had several break my four-pound-test lines with their mad rushes.

We fished the weed bed both morning and evening that day. And at the end, when the sun was aflame with red once more, setting into the tree-covered bluffs to the west, fifty of the scrappy bass had been deposited on ice in the big insulated cooler that Sprick carries in his boat to keep his catches fresh.

Filleted and frozen, the fish are destined for smoking by Bill Barton, using his secret ingredients. And they'll end up as hors d'oeuvres for a shorelunch at a muskie fishing outing that's coming up soon on the Chippewa Flowage.

They're going to be lip-smackin', finger-lickin' good.

....Thanks to a guy who knows the Mississippi.

Uncle Herb

Well, the first Saturday in December is coming up. Now, the first Saturday in December is always a monumental day for me. That's the date that I declare the ice fishing season to be officially open.

Sure! I can hear it now....guys saying, "Hey! I've been fishing already." I know that. Ice fishing got off to one of the earliest starts

"1949, the Author and Uncle Herb"

I've ever seen in these parts, in early November after we had those below zero nights right after the big snowstorm.

And I've sashayed out myself, tapping the new ice with my chisel as I slipped and slid my way. Caught a fair walleye too, which is always nice on the first outing.

But for me, ice fishing before deer season's over really doesn't count. Those trips are more like pre-season practice games in football or spring training in baseball. Ya gotta get deer season over before you get down to the serious stuff!

And that's where the first Saturday in December comes in. Over the years, I've learned, that by that date, I can usually depend on safe ice. It's then that I stop looking back at the deer season, and start looking ahead to the best sport of all, ice fishing.

I'm prejudiced! I admit it! I like my ice fishing! And those feelings go back a long time, close to sixty years, to winter days when I'd traipse along behind my Uncle Herb.

Uncle Herb was an avid ice fisherman, one I'd even call an ice fishing pioneer. Because, back in those 1930-times, winter fishermen were few and far between. Today, with more leisure time, four-wheel drive vehicles, power augers, and the excellent outdoor clothing available, ice fishing has become a very popular pastime.

But I'm digressing. Back to Uncle Herb.

I can see him now; a tall, robust man dressed in an old black overcoat, one that had outlived its best days of wear, to church on Sunday mornings and family card parties on Saturday nights. Under the coat was his red-and-black plaid woolen deer hunting suit, the one he'd bought at the woolen mill in Merrill once on a fishing trip up north; the breeches of which he tucked into four-buckle overshoes and felt shoes that served as his footwear.

Lake Montgomery was our favorite fishing grounds. Montgomery, in those times, was a jewel of a little lake. Not a building desecrated its shoreline, its edges lush with thick cattail marshes, home to all sorts of wild things. Not today. The last time I saw Lake Montgomery, its banks were riddled with cottages and homes, its marshes gone.

At an abandoned farm house, a quarter-mile or so from the lake, Uncle Herb would park his black Plymouth. And from its trunk, would come a peach basket containing his tipups, an ice chisel, and a pail of bait, either minnows or the dead "bloaters" that he'd get from the commercial fishermen on Lake Michigan.

Through the old pasture and into the cattails we'd walk; Uncle Herb carrying the valuable stuff, I the heavy steel chisel, something I couldn't damage if I tripped.

Often, over my shoulder, I carried my twenty-two rifle. And as we moved through the marsh, I'd eye the snow for tracks of cottontail rabbits, critters I'd pursue when the fishing action was slow.

Upon reaching the frozen lake, Uncle Herb would begin to set out his lines; chiseling holes in the ice, into which he'd peer, looking for "pickerel weeds." Find a spot that had good pickerel weeds, and there Uncle Herb would set a tipup, homemade from orange crate slats and umbrella staves, with wooden spools for reels.

The lines in, Uncle Herb would retreat to a sheltered bank, out of the wind. Wood gathering would be my job, and a fire built to warm us, toast our homemade bread sandwiches, and just plain add cheer to the day.

There we'd stand, talking, maybe fire a few rounds with the twenty-two, and wait for the red flag of a tipup to pop skyward. Let that happen, and across the ice we'd scurry to the lucky line. There, Uncle Herb would carry on a running narrative of what the fish was doing under the ice. And suddenly, with a wild flourish of his arms, he'd set the hook, hand-over-hand the line, and a fat northern pike would come flopping out of the hole onto the ice.

Over time, since those boyhood fishing days, I've repeated that experience literally hundreds of times with family and friends.

Uncle Herb's been gone many years now. Yet the memories he left with me of those beautifully wild and lonely long-ago ice fishing outings continue to linger strong.

....Come the first Saturday in December, I'll begin reliving them all over once again.

Tiny Bootprints

Tiny footprints etched in the snow. Tiny bootprints made by a grandson the day before, his three-year-old feet clad in miniature Sorels, boots his grandma had found at a rummage sale, and given to him for wear on his winter ice fishing trips. Cute little boots with warm felt liners, flashy yellow laces, and fringes of fuzzy sheepskin around their tops.

The meandering trails in the snow marked another chapter in a long saga of memories that surround a hallowed little corner of a lake where, in winters, our family has gathered to drill holes in the ice and set out our tipups.

I was aware that grandson and his dad had fished the spot the day before. I'd heard that they intended to be there. So I'd driven out on the frozen lake to check on the two. There, in the cab of the Jeep, snuggled in his warm snowsuit, soaking up sunshine, grandson sat, sipping a can of Squirt to wash down a sandwich he'd just finished.

He waved his hand to greet me, and I opened the door on the driver's side and partially slid myself onto the seat, next to him. "Want some of my pop, grandpa?" he'd asked, holding the can of soda out to me. "No thanks, Jesse," I'd answered; "I've got a bad cold and I wouldn't want you to catch it!"

The three of us stood and sat there quietly, visiting.

Nearby on the ice, laid a five pound northern pike they'd caught a short while earlier. Suddenly, up pops a red flag, and son and I take off in a trot to the lucky tipup. And as we get to it, looking back, we see two tiny feet sprouting from the Jeep's door, followed by a tiny body sliding out onto the frozen lake's surface.

"He's growing up faster than I figured," his dad said, as the youngster made his way across the ice toward us, leaving behind his trail of tiny footprints....not about to be left out of the action, that was obvious.

In short order, the two-foot-long northern pike came splashing out of the hole. And as it did its flip-flops on the ice, glistening green and yellow and white against the snow, Jesse picks up the gaff hook. Valiantly, he tries to impale the fish's snout. For he's got a job to do, that of dragging the fish back to the Jeep, a job he absolutely refuses to relinquish to anyone else. It's his job, and he's going to do it. And with a little hand from his dad, he does, proudly.

I'd left them there then, and headed home; satisfied with what I'd seen, savoring the emotions I'd felt. And later that night, the phone rang. "Have to tell you, dad, what happened after you left," son says, and proceeds to explain how Jesse, taking his turn with a tipup, had hooked into the biggest fish of the day, one that measured 32 inches long. "I had to give him a little help to bring it through the hole, but he landed it pretty much on his own," son told.

But the best part came as Jesse did his job of dragging the huge northern over to the Jeep. "That was quite a sight...a 36-inch boy pulling a 32-inch fish," son chuckled. Then, as grandson looked at his big fish lying next to the others, he'd turned and said, "You only catch the little ones, Dad!"

Words that I'll long remember. Words that I may never

forget. Words, like others, and sights and experiences that will keep coming back to me each time that I go back to that special little corner of my fishing world.

Memories like the day several years ago when son-in-law, daughter and their family were home from North Carolina for a Christmas. Three of us; son-in-law, son, and I had gone to that little corner to do some fishing.

I call it the day the northern pike went crazy! Never have I seen fish bite like they did that morning. Red flags popping constantly, and fish flopping on the ice. The three of us limited-out that day; fifteen northern pike that ran from four to eight pounds, the best catch of northern pike that I've ever been part of.

I sat there on that personal little fishing domain the other day, parked in my pickup with the low December sun beaming through the windows, watching my tipups frozen in suspended animation out front. And suddenly, out of nowhere, two bald eagles appeared, circling over my lines, wings outstretched, white tails spread fan-like, barely fifty yards in front of me, trying to muster the courage to swoop down to pick up the scraps of bait fish lying on the ice.

The sight of the two majestic birds so near was truly spectacular, another special moment.

But no more so, than the strings of tiny bootprints that laced the snow, left there by a little fisherman who had passed that way the day before....

And caught a big fish.

"Bill Barton and Big Chetac Perch"

A Boogered Finger

My old pal Bill.... "Prof Perch," I call him....Barton had me worried. The old professor is a living legend in the annals of perch fishing, you see. A lifetime he's spent in deep and reflective research on the subject of catching perch. Without a doubt, he's one of the world's renowned experts in the field.

I know because I've been privileged to sit in on a semester or two of his lectures, lessons that he's conducted in outdoor classrooms on frozen lakes all the way from here to Canada. Listen to the old prof expound at length on the data he's collected, the secrets he's uncovered in his years of study, and one comes away awestruck, humbled by the immensity of his knowledge.

But Old Prof had me uptight. The word was out that he'd boogered up a finger just before Christmas, while in the process of manufacturing a toy wooden wagon, a present for one of his grandchildren.

How serious was the injury? Would his fishing technique suffer? Would he be able to impart that 'just right' jigging action to the Swedish pimple bait on the end of his line? Would the razor-sharp reflexes still be there to set the hook at the slightest nip of a feeding perch? Could he, indeed, even handle his ultra-light rods and reels, gear that he's spent years field-testing and perfecting?

Those were the questions that were racing through my mind the other night as Momma and I paid a visit to the old prof and his wife, Evie.

There we sat in the living room of their cozy log home, jawing about the weather, the grandkids coming for Christmas, their itinerary for a trip south, everything but Old Prof's boogered finger.

Far be it for me to bring up the subject, I figured. Maybe the guy's as worried about his career, his life's work, his reputation as much as I was. Maybe he wasn't ready to talk about it yet. I understood.

But, just as I was about to concede, up he jumps from his favorite recliner and across the room he charges, to shake a left hand, five fingers extended, under my nose.

"See what I did to my finger!" he says, wiggling the middle one, the end of which looks sort of like a young mushroom; except that it's purple, has a criss-cross of stitch marks, and the fingernail is gone. "Same one I nicked two years ago," he goes on. "It's coming along OK though. The only bad thing about it is that it gets cold so easy!"

And then, almost as an afterthought, a bit defensively, he adds, "But it's not bothering my fishing!"

Well, I'll tell you those were beautiful words to hear, calming my concerns, reassuring me that the great man's career wasn't in jeopardy.

And almost impulsively, I said, "What're you doing tomorrow? Let's go down to Big Chetac and try the perch."

"OK by me," he came back. "What time can you be over?"

"Eight-thirty!" I answered.

And the next morning found the two of us easing along

the back roads of the Edgewater country, through hardwood-forested hills, the trees beautiful in a white sheathing of early morning hoarfrost.

"See this," the old prof says, waving a finger in the air, one that's encased in a yellow finger from an old glove. "That's to keep that thing warm!" Leave it to the old prof to think of a gadget like that, I figure.

Across the lake to one of his favorite fishing spots we drive. And there, after augering a couple dozen holes, the great man goes to work; the tiny innocent-looking graphite rod in his hands turning into a deadly weapon.

Like a good bird dog working pheasant cover, he goes about his business. First to the left, then to the right, he works the habitat, his nostrils straining for perch scent. And finally, he locks in on a productive hole.

"Oh-h-h!" he chuckles, "they're down there! Look at that one fight! Ain't he a beauty!"

And soon the ice around him is speckled with fat, flopping fish.

The sight is almost overwhelming. Gone is the fear that the man's career might be at an end. Gone is the apprehension that his image, one he'd created with a lifetime of toil and sacrifice, might be tarnished.

The old prof could still catch perch, that was for sure....boogered finger or not!

Old Guide

Gene Mommsen is 78 now. This winter he spent a lot of his time watching wildlife from the kitchen window of his tidy home overlooking Chicog Creek west of Minong. There the chickadees and bluejays, the gray squirrels and ruffed grouse, come to the feeders he keeps stocked with sunflower seeds and shelled corn.

And deer. "I had up to 21 in the yard at one time," he told me recently, as we sat sipping coffee.

But watching wildlife wasn't always Gene's life. For many years, he was a premier fishing and hunting guide in the Birchwood area.

"For twenty years, from 1946 to 1966, I had a camp on an island in Little Superior Lake," he reminisced. The lake lies deep in the heart of the Washburn County Forest. "I leased the land from the county," he went on. "At that time, you could do that. Today you can't."

I spent an afternoon with Gene the other day; a most pleasant afternoon, listening to stories of his guiding days; tales too numerous to squeeze into this column today, believe me.

"There was just a rough trail from the old logging days to the lake," he told. "I had two army-surplus 'Platypus' vehicles that I used for travel." The Jeep-like amphibious rigs were used in the South Pacific in World War II. "They could go anywhere on land or water," Gene added. "They had four-wheel drive for land and a water-tight hull with a rudder and a big brass propellor for water."

The camp was built from dead popple logs, trees that had died when the water level of the lake had risen. "They were hard as rock, and I used them for the rafters and studding. But my lumber came from Ted Hagg's fish boxes."

Hagg, at the time, operated the Sarona House supper club. "It was known all over the United States," Mommsen said. "He'd get shipments of fish from Sweden in the wooden boxes that I used for lumber."

Hagg and Mommsen were close friends. "Ted got all my customers for me. He guaranteed all my reservations up to October first each year," Gene said.

And to that camp, rustic and isolated, back in the wilds, the fishermen and hunters came. "Most were from Kentucky, Indiana, Ohio, and Illinois," Mommsen said. "They stayed up to a week. But usually I was booked so heavy I could only give them a day or two.

There, in a region that is dotted with small pristine lakes, Mommsen would guide his clientele to outstanding fishing. Bass fishing was his specialty.

"I always fished with artificial lures," he told. "And I always had an agreement with my customers, that if they didn't catch their limit they didn't have to pay for the guiding. I never had to pay off."

Once he came close, however. "I had a crew from Beloit out with me. I called them the 'bean sandwich gang.' Well, we couldn't get a hit along the shore, so I took them to a deep hole in the lake. There, the bass hit so hard that it kept me busy with the landing net. We ended up with twenty bass that ran from five to nine pounds. That was the best catch of fish I ever made."

And an interesting husband-and-wife fishing tale. "I picked them up at a motel. The wife had a nice tackle box and a fancy fly rod," Gene said with a smile. "But the husband told me to drop him off at a local bar, saying 'I hate fishing. You take my wife fishing!'"

"Well, the wife was a fishing fanatic! For two solid days she fished with that fly rod from morning to dark!"

In the fall, the hunters came for grouse. "Some had excellent dogs," Mommsen said. "I remember one named Queenie, that went clear across a forty to retrieve a wing-tipped bird."

Then, the deer seasons. "There weren't a lot of bucks back in there early in the season," Gene told. "So we took it easy then. But then the farmers around the outside of the area would start to make drives, and they'd push the deer back to us. The last four days of the season were always the best. One year I got a sixteen-pointer and a fourteen-pointer. But there were years when I got nothing too."

And some exciting adventures with his amphibious vehicles. Like the time, unknown to Gene, a hole got burned in one's hull. And upon making the trip to the island, it began to sink, forcing him to beach it.

And another experience while crossing a lake on ice. The vehicle broke through with a crash. And a passenger, unfamiliar with the rig, thought it was about to sink. "George jumped overboard," Gene chuckled, "onto the ice and broke his leg!"

Battling some health problems now, Mommsen doesn't spend a great deal of time in the outdoors any more. He did go back last summer to visit his old campsite, however.

"The cabin burned years ago," he mused. "There's not much to see now."

"But there's an awful lot of good memories!"

Jig Maker Supreme

The phone rang one day a couple weeks ago. I answered.
"This is Jim Farlik calling," the voice on the other end
announced. "Are you the guy that wrote that article in the
Woodsman magazine about making fishing jigs?"
"I'm the guy!" I came back.
"Well, I've been tieing jigs for over forty years. And I
think I could show you a few things," the voice continued.
Thus began an association with Jim Farlik, fishing tackle
maker ala professional. Next to him, my talents are raw ama-
teur, like a bush league baseball player compared to a major
leaguer.
On a recent Saturday, I spent an afternoon with the
Farliks, Jim and Frances, his wife, at their comfy home nes-
tled amongst the pines on Lower McKenzie Lake in northwest Washburn County. There the two seventy-somethings
have resided year-round since Jim's retirement fourteen
years ago from a life-long career as a barber in Chicago.
But, while barbering was his livelihood, another side of
Jim Farlik existed. He loved the outdoors, his hunting and
his fishing. And that love led him into a hobby of creating
fishing lures; a pastime that he pursued with a passion, so
fierce that he became a recognized expert in the field.
"Tieing flies was really my specialty," he said. "I had

booths at all the big sports shows in the Chicago area for many years. There I demonstrated fly-tieing. I appeared on Chicago television too. And I belonged to several of the better fly-tieing clubs, including the Northwest Fly Tie-ers of Arlington Heights."

The times were the 1940's and 50's, back when fishing with a fly rod was the ultimate mark of a sportsman, and tieing your own flies was part of that sport. With the advent of spinning rods and reels in the early 1960's, fly-fishing declined in popularity. Today, it's once again on the rise.

"I really got into making jigs by accident," Jim went on. "A friend of mine wanted to learn how to tie flies. I knew he was good at tieing jigs. So I told him 'I'll teach you how to tie flies, if you'll teach me how to tie jigs.'"

And with that, on to my own personal tutoring.

After a brief...and polite...inspection of a sample of lures I'd brought along, jigs I figure would catch walleyes, Jim began at square one.

First, instruction on the proper preparation of deer tails, from which the hair comes for jigs. The tails have to be thoroughly washed before they're dyed, something I thought I'd been doing a fair job at. Not quite. They should also be "degreased" said Jim, spelling out the procedure for doing so.

Next, the thread for the winding of the hair. Not the dime store variety I'd been buying. And a look in one of Jim's tackle supply catalogs for the brand he recommends. The same for the glues and vinyl paints he uses.

And finally, a demonstration of his skills and techniques. For three hours, broken only for a coffee break visit with Frances, we sat together there, next to the workbench where his English-made tieing vise was mounted.

I watched in true awe as his nimble fingers turned bare

hooks and deer hair, colored feathers called "hackle", and yellow and black strips of chenille into beautiful creations of fishing art.

And I listened carefully to all that he said, asked all the questions that crossed my mind. When my chance came to try my hand, the two jigs I tied were several times improved. As we ended our session, a handful of jigs were waiting for me to take home, lures that bear an unwritten "Made by Farlik" label.

Last, a show-me tour of the shop where he spends a lot of his winter days. On the walls, hung beautifully-crafted graphite fishing rods he builds, another of his talents. And from a cupboard, two boxes of cork bodies for 300 bluegill poppers he's making.

Hanging on Jim Farlik's wall were two largemouth bass he's caught; one over seven pounds, the other a tad smaller. "But I lost a bigger one, probably over eight pounds, right out in front of the house," he told.

The proof of the pudding is in the eating, it's been said.

The proof of Jim Farlik's bait-making skill hangs there on his wall, I'd say.

"Jim Farlik at his workbench"

Boat Safety

You say you've never had a boating accident! You say you've never even had a close call!

You're fortunate, believe me.

I have. Like the time I tipped my skiff while duck hunting and nearly drowned. Like the time I started my outboard motor in gear...and almost spun myself overboard. Like the time my partner rammed a stump one dark morning on the Wisconsin River, almost capsizing us.

And thanks, but no thanks, please! I want no more of those stupid, carelessly-caused experiences. The older I get, the more chicken I get when I'm on the water. And smile all you want, but that's the way it's going to stay!

Bart Halverson and I did some visiting recently about boating accidents. Halverson is DNR's law enforcement safety specialist at Spooner for northwest Wisconsin. It's his job, for example, to teach our kids how to handle guns, snowmobiles and boats safely, something he and his helpers do with instruction programs each year.

But we grown-ups can stand a little finger-pointing too, especially now that the fishing season is upon us. Last year, 1991, 23 people lost their lives in boating accidents on Wisconsin waters; of those deaths, 22 were by drowning.

"Standing up in the boat is the biggest cause," he said.

"Wisconsin DNR's Bart Halverson teaches boat safety"

"Early in the year, like now, water temperatures will be in the 40's. Fall overboard, and a person will be unconscious within ten minutes in that."

"I've seen fishing openers where there was ice floating," he continued. "You see fishermen dressed in snowmobile suits and Sorrel boots. Go over dressed like that, and you've had it."

"That tells you to wear a personal flotation device," he added. "PFD's and better yet, float coats, not only keep a person afloat, but they also protect against hypothermia. Any person who doesn't wear a PFD early in the season is really asking for trouble. PFD's would prevent seventy percent of our fatalities."

Wisconsin law requires a PFD for each person on board. And they must be Coast Guard approved, in serviceable condition, and readily accessible. "Our wardens like to see them out, not stuffed in a compartment," Halverson said.

Boats over sixteen feet in length, must have a wearable PFD for each passenger. "That means that if there are twenty people on a pontoon boat, there must be twenty wearable PFD's," he said. "In addition, such larger boats must also have a throwable preserver on board."

And another source of potentially serious accidents...storage batteries. With the advent of trolling motors, fish locaters, electric-start motors and running lights, a high proportion of boats now carry batteries.

"Fires can occur," Halverson said. "The battery terminals must be covered, and the battery secured so it can't move. That's the law."

"I've seen batteries almost touching the gas tanks. A wrench falls and arcs across the terminal, and you're going to have a fire. I wrote a ticket last year on a guy out in an old beat-up boat with three little girls on board in a situation just like that. The guy didn't know how close he was to having a fire."

Running lights should also be in good operating order, he said. Personally, I like to use my lights defensively when I'm fishing at night, switching them on when another boat nears.

"The law requires motorboats to have lights between sunset and sunrise," Halverson said. "Many people don't understand the reason for the two colors, red and green. A red light indicates a boat approaching from the right, for example. Always yield to a person on the right. If you see a red light coming, yield."

And lastly, some words on drinking and driving, a boat that is.

"Wisconsin has an implied consent law for boating, just as it has for driving a car on the highway," he said. "That means that if you're operating a boat, you have consented to being tested for being under the influence if there's probable cause." Recent studies have shown that alcohol hits a person harder and faster when boating because of the fresh air, sunshine and boat movement, he said.

So what does it all add up to?

Well, Wisconsin has about a million acres of lakes. It also has a half-million licensed boats. That's about two acres of water apiece were we all out there at the same time, not a heck of a lot! And that number's going down.

Bart Halverson said it all as he closed his safety message: "Use common sense. Be responsible!"

Fishing With Fred

Fred Patchin took me fishing the other day.

Fly fishing.

For bluegills.

We'd been talking about it for almost two years now. On summer evenings, when I'd be cutting the grass out front, sometimes Fred would drive by. He'd stop, holler out the window, "When we goin' fishin'?"

Oh, I knew about Fred and his fly-fishing. I'd seen him clad in his chocolate-brown chest-high waders, his straw hat perched firmly over his brow, standing waist-deep in the waters of Spooner Lake, as I passed on the way to my tree farm.

"I've been a fly fisherman since I was a boy," he told me the other day as I rode alongside him, headed for one of his favorite bluegill spots. "It's about the only kind of fishing I do anymore."

He's 77 now, retired for fifteen years, from a career in the banking business; a career that began in 1938. Summers he and his wife, Margaret, spend here in the north; the winters in Texas.

"You ought to see how fly-fishing is catching on in Texas," he told me. "There they have classes to teach it."

"Fly-fishing seems to be coming back all over," I

"Fred Patchin enjoys fly fishing for Bluegills"

responded. "Back when I was a boy, you had three kinds of fish poles: a bamboo pole, a steel bait casting rod, and if you were a true sportsman, a fly rod."

But then, after World War II, spinning rods and reels hit the market; and fly-fishing all but disappeared. And I was no less guilty, as I allowed my fly rods to hang, unused, in the basement.

There was a time though, when I thoroughly enjoyed my fly-fishing. Years back, when we lived in Tomahawk, I got pretty good at catching bass on big popper baits. Then at Park Falls, on a pretty little lake out in the woods, I'd wade the shoreline, casting dry flies for rainbow trout. And in the 60's, White Clay Lake near Shawano gave up its share of fat bluegills to my red-and-white poppers on hot summer nights.

I'd almost forgotten how much fun it was to have a fish swirl at a dainty lure, how much bend a scrappy bluegill could put into a flimsy fly rod.

Until the other day, that is.

"What kind of a fly do you recommend," I'd asked Fred, as we began our wading. "I like one that I call a bumble bee," he'd answered.

And with that he began his casting, laying out his line smoothly, gracefully. I knew he'd cast well. But I wasn't too sure about my own abilities. It'd been a long time.

Cautiously, tentatively, I began my own fishing, checking my back casts for overhanging branches along the shore. Fly-casting requires coordination between the fisherman; his rod, reel, and line; and most of all, his environment.

But the old rhythm quickly came back. "Fly-fishing must be like riding a bicycle," I yelled to Fred. "Once you learn it, you never forget it!"

And I began to relax, to enjoy the afternoon.

Some days are pretty, some days are beautiful. Our day was a combination of both; warm sunshine wafting down between puffs of white clouds floating on a blue sky. Underfoot, the lake's bottom felt soft and squishy to my booted toes. Lacy fronds of green waterweeds, curly white snail shells, and pincer-like clam shells decorated the sand and mud in the crystal-clear water.

Up the shore, a pair of mallard ducks dabbled for food. And around a point, a pair of loons yodelled up a storm. In the rushes on the water's edge, bullfrogs croaked a husky chorus.

"It doesn't look like the big ones are in yet," Fred announced as we worked our rods. Small 'gills, yes. We could see them flitting in the shallows. But the large spawning fish, no.

Still the action was good enough for me. After all, I'd come to watch an expert fish. Then secondly, to recapture a bit of my long-lost fishing past.

I found it too! At the edge of a smattering of lily pads. There I cast my tiny yellow cork popper, retrieving it ever so slowly, making little "plip" sounds with it on the still water.

There the hand-sized sunfish came to strike, their back fins swirling the surface; to slice the water, silvery and blue, as they fought.

I didn't catch all that many. And those I did, went back into the lake. But that was OK.

Fred and I plan to go again next week, you see.

Muskie Memories

The muskie, stung by the hook in its jaw, plunged deep into the lake's depths, ripping, line from the fisherman's reel, its body gleaming emerald green in the clear water....

Muskie fishing memories!

Fish a lake for twenty-five years and one acquires a rich bundle.

And another was in the making.

The lake? Big Sissabagama, it's called; its name as long and complicated as the green-eyed, black-hearted heathen fish that it grows. I know, because I've spent my share of hours heaving hairy bucktails to its rocky reefs, retrieving sputtering surface baits over its fern-like weedbeds.

John Plenke and I spent a day on Big Sis recently. Plenke, an old hunting and fishing buddy, was back in these parts for a Wisconsin vacation. He now lives in Montana.

And while we shivered under rain gear in a wet wind-driven cold, we talked the kind of talk that fishermen talk.

He told me, for instance, about his elk hunting adventures up in the Bitterroot Mountains last fall. How a big bull sped past him; its antlers laid back, preventing a look for a brow point, which would have made the animal legal; forcing John to pass on his one chance to fill his tag.

He spoke of his trout fishing on the Gallatin and Madison

Rivers, where the rainbows and browns grow large, streams so icy cold from melting mountain snows that fishermen wear wet-suit type waders to survive, should they get swept off their feet.

Talk like that's powerful, competition that's hard to meet. And the best I could do, was to share some of my Big Sis memories, tales of muskie fishing days long gone by.

"Right here, I once saw two legal muskies caught on two consecutive casts," I told as we worked our way along a reed-fringed rock bar. "Dave Jacobson caught one and Milt Deickman the other, one evening years ago."

But no such luck for us. And across the lake to drift a weed-speckled bar. There Plenke told of the big Canadian honkers that come to the decoys he sets out on a lonely little mountain lake.

And I told of a 1979 time...the day I had Dave Begel fishing in my boat with me.

"Dave was a sports writer for the Milwaukee Journal," I began. "He'd come up with Jay Reed to do some muskie fishing. We'd fished for two days without much success."

"Well, right about here Dave was casting a black surface bait, when a really fine muskie struck. The fish hit so hard that it actually hooked itself. But the drag on Dave's reel jammed. He couldn't give line; and with the fish thrashing wildly, it finally broke the line."

On steadily, we fished into the evening dusk, ragged dark clouds passing overhead, taking their turns at pelting us with cold rain drops, that rattled off our hood-covered heads and stung our faces.

And another of my memories, one that goes back to Momma's fishing days.

"Marian and I were over here one Sunday afternoon," I

told. "Right over there off the tip of that island, she hooked a muskie. Well, let me tell you she was plenty excited as she played it. She did a good job, and after a few minutes, I netted it. She was really proud of herself."

"Well, I unhooked it and laid it on the yard stick screwed to the center boat seat for a measurement. This was back in the thirty-inch size limit days. Well, the fish measured a quarter-inch short, and without a second thought, I dropped it over the side. You should have seen the look she gave me! I don't think she's forgiven me to this day!"

....One more pass over some good water, a last cast, a final retrieve, and my day with Plenke came to an end.

Yet snapped to the memory stringer in my mind was a special muskie.

The fish had risen off the deep side of a bar to hit my bucktail. It fought a valiant battle. Measured at 34 inches, it was no keeper, yet still a nice fish.

And you can believe it's properly logged into my mental muskie memory book.

The one I caught with John Plenke, I'll call it.

Boys, Bobbers and Bluegills

Boys, bobbers and bluegills...they're made for each other. I guess I've known that for many years. But it doesn't hurt to refresh one's thinking now and then.

Take a kid fishing, the sign outside the sports shop had said. The message couldn't have been more appropriate.

For our two North Carolina grandkids were "home" for a visit with Grandma and me, something neither they nor we get to do too often. And on the agenda were all kinds of good things; like spending time with their cousins, backyard picnics, swimming, and as in the case of teen-age Michelle, "doing some serious shopping."

Not eleven-year-old Ben, however. His priorities were different. "I'm looking forward to some good fishing with you," he'd told me over the phone the weekend before the pair's plane trip north. And he'd repeated that wish during the car ride from the Minneapolis airport.

Even his folks had warned me. "Ben wants to go fishing more than anything else," they'd said. That of course, was music to my ears. A grandpa likes to see a grandson with his priorities straight.

And I'd done my homework. I was ready for him. After all, I've had a little experience taking eleven-year-olds fishing. In fact, if I try real hard, I can recall the excitement I knew myself, when I was that age, and a benevolent uncle would give up his Sunday afternoon to take me fishing.

Bluegills, it would be for our first outing. "We'll start with the small stuff and build up to the big ones," I told Ben. For good reasons. Bluegills usually mean fast action. And that's important to a boy with fishing on his mind.

Then, I picked a lonely little lake that sets off all by itself in the boondocks, a place where the two of us could be by ourselves. Where the wonders of our north country, trees and birds and bullfrogs, all blend together in a way I hoped he'd remember...and maybe look back to some day in his years ahead.

There, we dropped the boat in at the little landing. There, I snapped a tiny red-and-white bobber to his line and gave my advice on how to thread a piece of wiggly nightcrawler onto a hook.

I watched as he prepared to cast with the light spinning rod I'd rigged for him. "Grandpa," he asked, "do you still have that old cane pole I used to use?"

"Yes, I do," I answered, and I realized that perhaps I should have brought it along. Boys have fond memories of old bamboo fishing poles.

His first cast landed only a short distance from the boat. Reeling in, he tried again. This time he laid his baited line perfectly at the edge of the lily pads. Almost immediately the tiny bobber twitched and disappeared beneath the water's surface. The scrappy hand-sized bluegill gave him a good tussle as he worked it to the boat. Lifting it over the side, the fish was his first for the stringer.

Between my own casts, I watched him as he fished. And it dawned on me how differently kids fish compared to grown-ups. With grown-ups too often a fish is just a fish.

Hurry up and catch another.

Not with kids. There's the quiet contemplation of the fish's anatomy, the size of its eyes, its colors. There's the patience of slowly unraveling a snarl of line on the end of the pole, or a backlash in the reel. There's the slow deliberateness of freeing a hook from the anchor rope and the skittish reluctance of picking up a flopping, sharp-finned critter.

We caught a nice mess of bluegills the other day, Ben and I. And that night, after he'd been given a lesson in filleting, Grandma served a batch, golden brown, for supper.

He'd enjoyed the day, he said.

The same held for me. And more.

I'd watched a boy fish again. And I'd learned something about values, something that I might have misplaced along the way. That a half-pound bluegill can mean as much fishing fun as a twenty-pound muskie.

It's all in the way you look at it.

Catfish Are His Specialty

Catfish is spoken here today!

Pete Stafford took me fishing for catfish recently. Pete Stafford understands catfish language. So much so that I'd call him a catfish expert, at least here in these northwestern Wisconsin parts. He catches catfish, big ones.

And that's unusual, because here in our water-rich region of lakes and streams are found bountiful populations of bass, walleyes, muskies, northern pike, trout and panfish; species that attract the attention of thousands of fishermen each year; species that get all the glory, all the publicity.

But the catfish? Whoever heard of it? Heck! They're the critters that live "down South," where the catfish is king. Catfish on the menu is standard fare in southern restaurants.

And that uniqueness caught my ear when I heard about Stafford and his fishing specialty. When the opportunity came for me to join him on one of his outings, I jumped at the chance.

We'd fish the Clam River below the dam at the lower end of Clam Lake, he said, as we met at his home in eastern Burnett County. But first, a look at a photo album, pictures of fish that he's caught in recent years.

"I heard about the big catfish in the Clam River in 1984," he said. "That's when I started fishing for them. That year, I caught one that weighed 26 1/2 pounds."

And he and catfish have been hooked, so to speak, on each other ever since.

"This year so far, I've taken nineteen that weighed more than ten pounds each," he added. "The biggest one I've caught weighed 39 1/2 pounds. I caught it two years ago. But I've had one on that I know would go 45 to 50 pounds. I fought that fish for 45 minutes before it broke my line right at the net."

Upon our arrival at the Clam Dam, Stafford explained his fishing technique. His fishing is done from the bank in the pool below the dam.

He uses stout spinning rods equipped with reels that are loaded with plenty of fifteen-pound test line. His hooks are a special brand called "Tru-Turn." They're shaped so that they'll rotate when he sets the hook.

For bait, he uses large dead shiner minnows secured from the Yellow River near his home. The minnows are threaded onto the long-shanked hook with the point imbedded near the tail. "That cuts down on the snags," he said. A small buckshot-size sinker is pinched onto the line a foot above the hook.

Casting out the baited lines, the rods are placed in rod holders at the water's edge. And the wait for fish action begins, signalled by a dipping and twitching of a rod tip. With a comfortable bench to sit on, one of several in the little park at the dam, the fishing is comfortable, casual and relaxed.

"I fish two or three times a week," Pete told me, "depending on the weather. Hot weather seems to be the best, and I've had my best fishing right in the middle of the day."

I asked Stafford about the eating qualities of catfish. "I fillet them out just like I do a walleye," he said. "So they're boneless. The bigger ones, say over ten pounds, are best smoked. A neighbor of mine, Joe Boyle, does mine. The smaller ones are good both baked and fried."

As the late afternoon turned to darkness, Stafford was apologetic about the lack of strikes. He'd had a fish on for a brief moment before his line became snagged in the rocks and logs that mark the river's bottom. A cold front had gone through earlier in the day with thunder booming and lightening flashing. I blamed that. Cold fronts don't help fishing, I've found.

Still the hours had been pleasant. Several acquaintances of Pete's stopped by to check on how things were going. Nearby young boys fished for crayfish in the rock rip-rap. And through it all came the music of the river, the sound of its water rippling over the dam's spillway.

There's always a next time. And the dream of another mammoth catfish.

"When I catch another really big one, I'll have it mounted," Pete said. "Some people say they're ugly things."

"But to me, they're beautiful!"

Trade River Trout

The world was peaceful there, in the valley of the Trade River. Don West and I were fishing for trout...and enjoying the immense beauty and solitude that surrounded us.

But Don was worried. I could tell. Except for an occasional chub, a couple of suckers, and a baby walleye that somehow had found its way into the river, the fish weren't biting.

"This is the lowest I've ever seen the water," Don commented as we worked our way upstream; he hugging the bank in hip boots, I wandering all over in my waders. Low water usually makes for tough trout fishing.

The Trade, in western Polk County, is one of West's favorite streams. And he'd issued an invitation to me to join him. "The stream doesn't hold a lot of trout," he'd cautioned me. "But the ones you do catch are nice. I've had fish on that would go five-six pounds."

And that was what was bothering Don. Invite a guy to go fishing and, every time it seems, the fish refuse to cooperate. I know the feeling, believe me. I've gone through the experience many times.

And I tried to convince Don that catching fish was secondary. "Don," I told him, "In my lifetime, I've caught my share of fish. Just being out here on this beautiful day, on this beautiful stream, that's what's really important."

Patiently, casually, we picked our way along the river, hopscotching past each other as we worked the deep holes and fast runs. The Trade is a big stream, one that meanders back and forth, criss-crossed with downed trees that have fallen into the river. To an experienced trout fisherman, almost every foot of it appears to have the potential to hold trout.

But, some pieces of water hold special promise. Like the fast deep run that curved under the overhanging foliage of a maple tree. For me, the milky, green water almost smelled of trout. And instinctively I approached the run with caution, positioning myself to make a perfect cast.

My nightcrawler-baited hook landed upstream, just above the leafy maple branches. The stream's current seized the worm, carrying it swirling downstream.

I felt the gentle tap-tap as a fish picked the bait from the bottom, and I set the hook. "There's one, Don!" I yelled, as the husky foot-long brown trout leaped once, twice, three times; its brown-and-orange-dotted silver sides flashing in the sun.

"That makes the trip," I said, as I slid the fish onto a sand bar.

"Well, I'm glad you caught one," Don came back, the worried look on his face gone. "It was beginning to look like I didn't know what I was talking about!"

The pressure was off! One fish, a fish that's caught at the right time, in the right place, can turn a fishing trip around, you see.

Then a trout for Don.

The fish came from under a tangle of debris that had lodged at the edge of a deep hole. Skillfully, he'd drifted his baited hook past the trout's hiding place.

From downstream, I heard the fish splash and saw the bend in Don's rod. "He's wrapped around something," he said as I hurried to help. In the two-foot water, I could see the struggling trout. And carefully I eased my hand along Don's line to free it.

Just under sixteen inches, the brown measured; a strong two-pounder, a very nice fish. "But they come bigger than that," Don commented, as we admired the handsome fish.

Mid-afternoon approached, time to wind the day down. And a last fish. A chunky thirteen-inch brown that came again from swift water flowing in the shade of a leaning tree, a place tailor-made for trout.

West and I had covered close to a mile of the Trade, I figured; counting all of its crooks and curves. It'd been a long time since I'd fished more beautiful water.

And through it all was the solitude, an almost over-powering silence broken only by two airplanes that had passed overhead, the call of a pileated woodpecker, the sound of our voices, and the music of the rippling river.

It's nice to know that places like that still exist.

The Gods of Fishing Fate Smile

The gods that decide the fates of hunters and fishermen know their business, I say. When they roll the dice to determine who's to come up winners, and who's to be losers, they usually bless the right people, I figure.

Take deer hunting, for example. Every year we hear stories about the youngster, barely in his or her teens, that's placed on a stand by dad and told to stay there until he returns, which may be the next week for all the poor kid knows.

But the young hunter follows instructions and sits there obediently, on a log. And a half hour later, a twelve-point buck walks up, stands broadside, while the youngster removes his mittens, takes long and careful aim, and downs the trophy beast with a single shot through the heart.

Same thing with fishing. I've had it happen to me.

Years ago, I'd take my boy, rigging a bamboo pole for him to catch crappies. One night he caught a seven-pound walleye. And the next, a four pounder...on crappie minnows and a bobber!

And daughter! When she tagged along, she always caught the most fish. Son would get so envious and jealous and mad, that he'd liked to have dumped her over the side of the boat.

So I'm kinda of the opinion that, somewhere upstairs, in that great sport shop in the sky, someone's pulling the strings when it comes to catching fish or bagging game.

Like the other night, for instance.

The phone rang. Joe Weiss was on the line. Joe's one of the guys I get to fish with a couple times a year. That is, when he gets time off from his job as an airline pilot, from flying to exotic places like the Caribbean Islands and Hawaii.

"Whatcha doin'?" he asked. "Been fishin'?"

Well, it turned out that he hadn't been ice fishing yet this winter. And to make a long story short, plans were made to join up the next day, for a try at the northern pike.

Keep in mind now, that this is the guy's first ice fishing outing of the season. And, as he told me later, it would also be his last for some time, what with having to spend several weeks soon in school, brushing up on the technology of flying DC-10's.

To Clam Lake near Siren, we'd go; a lake where I have great faith in my northern pike catching ability. And a lake to which I'll take partners when I want to better their chances of catching fish.

The morning drive to the lake went well, passing quickly, as we exchanged muskie fishing and deer hunting talk. And by 9:30, we had our tip-ups in the water, six lines baited with dead smelt. To the pickup we retired, out of the drizzle and sleet that was falling.

A half-hour passed, and up pops the flag on one of Joe's Arctics. "Right on cue," I said, as we trotted out to the lucky line. "Always seems to take a half-hour for the first bite after drilling the holes."

And in short order, the hook is set and a two-foot northern is flopping in the snow. "Well, it's always nice to catch the first one the first time out," Joe remarked.

Back to the truck we return, and before long up jumps another Weiss flag. Joe handles the fish expertly, and soon a twin to the first comes splashing from the hole.

All the while, I'm eyeing my own lines, standing dead in the water, wondering when my turn will come. And after Joe pulled a third pike from the lake, I even got desperate, cutting new holes and moving those dead-as-doornail tipups.

But to no avail. My day it wasn't. Except for one little dinker pike that I threw back, I was snake-bit.

Not Weiss, however. His hot hand continued. And by the time the lunch sandwiches were finished, he'd hung his fourth and fifth fish. His limit!

And I? Zip! Zilch! Zero!

That was the way it was intended to be, I decided. The guy deserved those fish, and the gods of fishing fate had smiled on him.

...and frowned on me.

"Dave Jacobson and a winter-caught Northern Pike"

Fun While It Lasted

It was fun while it lasted! Believe me!

Dave Jacobson, like a lot of fishermen this winter, was frustrated. His fishing had fallen on hard times, he'd declared. Old familiar bays and weedbeds, secret haunts that had produced big northern pike for him in past years, had gone dead; sending him home at the end of the day shaking his head in wonder and disappointment.

And not much better for me. Long hours, I'd spent staring at lifeless tipups, at tiny bobbers floating innertly on the waters of holes I'd drilled in the ice. A strong half-dozen outings had resulted in my bringing home barely enough fillets to stink up the pan, as the old-timers used to say.

That was the gist of the conversation the other morning as the two of us headed the pickup toward one of our favorite lakes. Something was strangely wrong with the behavior of fish this year, we agreed. And it had Jacobson uptight, so uptight that he was threatening to throw in the sponge; to head out to New Mexico to loll in the sun, amidst sagebrush, jackrabbits and rattlesnakes.

Overhead a thick layer of dark clouds hung as we drove, the kind of weather we seem to have had almost constantly of late.

"Maybe we need some of that southern sunshine here,

Dave," I said. "Maybe all this cloudy weather has reduced the oxygen levels in the lakes."

"I'd sure like to see some. I'm sick of this stuff!" Dave came back. Jacobson's not a lover of cloudy weather, especially in January.

As we drove, and as fate would have it, over the horizon began to peek a band of blue. And by the time we'd finished driving out to our fishing spot, a strong winter sun was beaming down from a cloud-free blue sky. From the west, blew barely a whisper of a breeze.

"What a day!" Jacobson said. "This is more like it!"

And with each of us manning our power augers, we began to set out our tipups, lines baited with smelt. Jacobson would set out two, and try for bluegills with a light jigging pole, which meant that he was in business ahead of me. There he sat on his little sled, twitching a teardrop, while I finished rigging my lines.

"Bob!" he hollered, pointing to one of my tipups, its flag fluttering proudly in the air. The line hadn't been in the water more than five minutes, and to it, I trotted. A brief wait, the hook set, and onto the ice skidded a respectable northern; no bragger, just a good-eatin'-size three-pounder.

"That's a good omen!" Dave yelled.

Well, I wasn't quite so optimistic, having been aced out so often recently.

The clock on the dashboard read a little after ten, as I settled down in the pickup, pouring myself a cup of coffee and tuning in a good George Jones tape of country western songs on the tape deck.

Fifteen minutes and Jacobson joined me, giving up on the bluegills. Bang! Up flips one of his flags, and the excited adrenaline rush as the two of us gallop out, slipping and sliding in the foot-deep snow. Dave does his job, and a second pike is history.

To the truck, we return. There I replace George Jones with a Garrison Keillor tape, a Christmas present from Johnny Walker. And as I'm chuckling to one of Keillor's tales, up pops another Jacobson flag. Adroitly, swiftly, Dave handles the fish, and northern number three is in the bag.

Then, with the fish barely on the ice, another of his lines springs skyward; and fish number four is flopping, green and yellow, in the snow.

"You know, we might just limit out here today," Dave said, a big smile showing. "This is the best fishing I've had all year."

And I began to agree with him, as the morning passed and the hot action continued. As noon closed in on us, and we sat munching sandwiches, two hits in quick succession on my tipups, added two more northerns to our catch. A total of six, the most I'd seen in one day this season.

And Dave's speculation about limiting out began to take on new potential. Surely with a full afternoon of prime fishing time ahead, in brilliant warm sunshine, we had a good chance of catching those last four pike.

But not to be. If anyone ever figures out what triggers a feeding spree by fish, or what causes them to shut down completely; well, that'll be the end of the sport of fishing.

For the rest of the day we sat there, talking, listening to Jones and Keillor; and except for two undersized northerns which we released, we caught not another keeper.

It'd been fun though.

And Jacobson's holding off on his trip to New Mexico.

Bow String Lake Perch

Bill Barton and I have a real knack for picking fishing weather.

I've been with my old pal, whom I refer to as "Prof Perch", when subzero cold and blizzard winds punished us in the wilds of Canada. And I've sat in the bow of his boat on Mille Lacs Lake over in Minnesota when the waves were so high I thought I'd be pitched over the side.

I've hunkered, clad in double rain suits on the Mississippi River as buckets of rain pelted down, drenching me to the skin. And I've suffered on breeze-less dead-calm lakes in broiling-hot suns that seemed to fry my brain.

So I guess I was naive recently when the two of us headed north on a perch fishing expedition.

Bill had called. "How about making a run up to Winnibigosh?" he'd asked. Winnibigosh is a lake in northern Minnesota. Barton has made a bundle of journeys there over the years. In fact, it was there that I first pinned the label of "Prof Perch" on him, as I'd listened to one of his seminars on the fine arts of catching perch.

"Sure, let's go," I told him; though in my mind, I'd pretty well closed the season on ice fishing. Yet, the thought of getting away for a few days to celebrate the end of winter and see some different country, sounded good.

And that night I did a little checking with a fellow fisherman that I know also goes to the Winnibigosh area. Yes, he said, the perch were hitting on Winnie. But another nearby lake, Bow String, was also producing.

Armed with that news, the next afternoon Barton and I hit the highway. Outside, the day was warm, sunny, springlike.

Four hours later found us at a bait shop in Deer River, Minnesota buying licenses and a supply of minnows. Checking into a motel, we quickly changed into our fishing clothes. We'd do some exploring, get organized for the next day when we planned to be on the ice at daylight.

Check out Bow String first, we decided. Finding our way into an access landing, we paused to survey the scene in front of us. It wasn't pretty. The trail onto the ice was rutted mud, and the lake's surface was a mass of deep slushy tire tracks where four-wheel drives had churned their way. Still, in the distance we could see the black specks of the fishermen's vehicles.

The mile drive out was rough going as the pickup bucked and bounced. But we made it, spilling only one pail of minnows. And the sight of fishermen pulling perch, hand over hand, from the lake got our adrenaline pumping.

Holes were drilled, lines were lowered, and Barton swung into action. The guy had seven plump perch flopping on the ice before I caught my first. As usual, Old Prof was in good form.

We fished until dark, leaving the lake excited about prospects for the next morning. We'd picked up some groceries. Our plan was simple. Thermoses of coffee would be made in the motel room, breakfasts and lunch would be eaten on the ice. We'd fish all day.

Dawn found us once more bouncing across the lake to our

fishing holes, marked by a stick in the ice. We were alone, the only fishermen out.

And the fish cooperated. For a half hour I struggled to finish a bowl of breakfast cereal, interrupted repeatedly by big chunky perch, some a foot long and weighing a pound, that yanked at my lines. Nearby Barton was doing even better, littering the ice around him with fish.

But then, the Becker-Barton weather syndrome struck once more. Slowly, a soft rain began to fall. Not hard, just enough to wet us down. But enough to take the fun out of things. All day, it fell. Twice I retreated into the truck.

Not Old Prof. He toughed it out. But by late afternoon, even he'd had his fill. And we headed in to dry out, and to replenish our minnow supply.

From the bait shop operator, we got the bad news, the weather forecast. Rain throughout the night, then turning to snow, with high winds!

We were snake-bit again! I should have known! The next morning, I awoke to find the door locks frozen on the pickup, as a stiff wind out of the north buffeted the pines and popples. And we headed for home, scrubbing the second day of the trip.

But in the back of the truck rested three pails that held a nice bunch of perch, now frozen tightly in the ice chips we'd packed them in. The trip had been a good one...even though the weather had clobbered us again!

We'd be back, we agreed...this summer, with a boat. We both want to fish Bow String again.

When the weather's nice...hopefully!

The Icemen Cometh!

"The Icemen," they've come to call themselves.

The label comes from a tradition they've established over the years, that of gathering in mid-November each year for one last fling at fishing before winter ice closes over their lake. I've been along on some of those outings, and they're brutal, marked by cold winds, snowflakes flying and ice chunks bouncing off bows of boats.

And we gathered again recently, six of us in all, anxious to work the kinks out of our casting arms, to relish to the roll of a boat riding gentle waves, to enjoy again the tug of a fish battling a rod.

Yet, there we were, standing frustrated, gazing out forlornly at a gray-white mass of foot-thick ice floes. Ice! Sure we expected, and accepted, the stuff in November. But this was late April! This was spring! The stuff was supposed to be gone!

The trip is an annual affair. Dick Birkholz is in charge. And each year, as winter gasps its last, and spring begins to stir, he leads us across Michigan's wondrous Upper Peninsula to L'Anse, a long arm of water that extends westerly off the main body of Lake Superior.

There at L'Anse, the Falls River and other nearby streams dump their waters into the bay. Attracted by that warmer

"Tom Kullman's Coho Salmon came from Lake Superior off L'anse, Michigan"

water, hordes of silvery smelt come to spawn in late April. And right behind them come the coho and king salmon, the brown and rainbow trout, big fish eager to partake of smelt dinners.

And that was why we fishermen had come, to cast our lures, hopefully in front of those hungry trout and salmon.

But the gods of fishing fates were working against us. On our arrival, out of the northeast, a stiff wind was blowing, pushing pack ice in off Lake Superior, plugging the entire Keweenaw Bay from L'Anse to Baraga. And we spent the first afternoon, futily looking for a landing where we could get our boats onto open water.

As darkness fell that first night, things looked dismal. Our only hope was for a windshift to the west, one strong enough to move the ice out toward the big lake once more.

Somewhere, sometime that night, someone must have said the right prayers. Because, come dawn as we rolled out for breakfast, there was the change in wind direction we needed. A quick inspection trip by Tom Newcomb to the harbor brought back the good word that there was enough open water to get our boats out.

And in short order, that was what we did; Tom Kullman and I riding in Newcomb's boat. And Johnny Walker and Mike Walsh in Birkholz's.

"Watch for ice chunks," Newcomb yelled to me sitting in the bow seat, as he maneuvered toward the open water in the distance. A three-mile run, and we began our fishing.

Overhead a leaden sky hung, threatening to open up with rain any minute. From the west, a steady cold breeze blew, and I was glad I was wearing a good ration of warm clothing.

Tieing on heavy, fast-sinking metal lures, we began our

fishing. We'd drift down wind, casting and retrieving, over water from twenty to forty feet deep. Newcomb's fish locator graph was marking fish almost constantly. The fish were present, that was obvious. But get 'em to bite, that would be the trick.

In the sky, loose strings of migrating ducks; golden-eyes, buffleheads, and mergansers circled. Screeching white gulls wheeled, loons sped by, adding a touch of springtime splendor to the scene.

And the first fish, a foot-and-a-half coho that smacked my orange and gold Little Cleo bait. Not big, just a "good eater." One fish in the live box is a lot better than none, Newcomb announced. And I agreed, especially when it's the first fish of a new season.

All day, except for a break to warm ourselves with hot coffee and cheeseburgers at a local eatery, conveniently located adjacent to the harbor, we fished. And when quitting time came late in the afternoon, the six of us had boated seven coho salmon. Not bad.

Add in the coho caught by Johnny Walker, and the seven-pound trout landed by Dick Birkholz, the next morning, and the catch became respectable.

And as the handshakes were exchanged and the goodbyes were said at the landing, plans were already being made for upcoming trips.

The ice will surely cometh again. That's certain.

But so will the Icemen.

Yellow River Float Trip

There I was, squinched down in the bottom of the boat, trying hard to make myself small. Up ahead, hanging out over the river, was a big tree; its top blocking most of the channel, its thick trunk barely four feet above the water's surface. And through that narrow niche our boat had to pass, hopefully with me and Charlie still aboard if it did.

Forward, relentlessly, the pull of the river carried us. And in a blurry couple of seconds, it was over. With a thud, as the boat careened against the tree's trunk, we burst through the opening, broken twigs and shreds of bark dusting our backs and shoulders.

Charlie Tollander and I were on a float trip down the Yellow River north of Webster, our purpose being to relieve the river of some of its burden of walleyes. And the tree blocking the river had added a touch of ominous, too-close-for-comfort excitement.

The trip was Charlie's idea. The plan had been to fish Yellow Lake, but a westerly gale was kicking up king-size white caps. "How about going down the river instead?" Charlie had proposed. "Fine with me," I'd answered. "It's been a long time since I've had a fishing float trip!"

And right after lunch on that warm, sunny afternoon, we'd dropped his light fourteen-foot boat into the Yellow at

"Charlie Tollander prepares to try the Yellow River for Walleyes"

a landing alongside Highway 35. Mounted on its stern was Charlie's trusty 5 1/2 horse outboard. "It's an old-timer," he chuckled. "It's a 1959, and it's known every rock in the St. Croix."

A quick run to spot Charlie's pickup and trailer at our takeout point, a return in my truck, and we were ready to shove off.

Quickly the river grabbed us. Its water was on the high side from recent rains, and its current had muscle. And as we passed under an old railroad trestle, civilization began to vanish.

"It's really a wild river," Charlie commented, as we slipped along. And he was right. Except for an airplane over-head, and some cattle bellowing in the distance, the world around us was unspoiled, untouched, as it's been for thou-sands of years.

Mistakenly, I'd assumed the run to Yellow Lake wasn't all that far, by map no more than a couple miles. Not by river! Measure all the crooks and curves, and it's gotta be closer to five, I came to learn.

But we'd come to fish. Our attack would concentrate on the bends where the river had cut deep holes. There we'd cast our jigs and Rapalas, hoping hungry walleyes lurked, eager to accommodate us.

Now, there's no substitute for experience when it comes to fishing strange waters. Charlie promptly proved that. Anchoring on a hole where a dead elm had toppled into the water, he quickly hooked two walleyes, both too small to keep. And I, after some finagling, finally boated a respectable smallmouth, also released.

That's the way the afternoon went. Float downstream, anchor on a hole, and fish it. Though Charlie put a good keeper walleye on the stringer, and several more small fish were released, the action was slow.

Little did I realize that the best of the day laid ahead. And catching fish would be only a small part of that experience.

Late afternoon, as the sun was about to touch the tree-shrouded horizon, and Charlie announced "Let's head for the lake." We'd fish the mouth of the river there, into the evening.

Let me say here that our slow, leisurely trip downstream was something to behold. Spring was in the air, and a blush of fresh green clothed the woods and marshes through which we passed. And the river was alive with wildlife. Around every bend, green-headed mallad drakes flushed. Awkward blue herons, an eagle. And a pair of long-necked, magnificent Canada geese. A variety of songbirds frolicked in the alders and willows. Overhanging it all, was an aura of peace and tranquility.

And finally, the wide expanse of marshland that marks the delta where the river enters the lake.

There, with Charlie guiding, we slipped slowly downstream, anchoring to work fast runs of deep water against the banks. And there we filled out our six-fish limit of walleyes, nice fish in the two-to-three pound class.

A run across the lake to our take-out point. And the day was over. Almost seven hours, we'd spent on the Yellow, and I was tired, beat, sunburned. But the trip was one I'll never forget.

"It's been a good day!" Charlie said over our goodbye handshake.

And that said it all.

A Trip Worth Waiting For

"Let's go fishing sometime," Owen Anderson had said. And "Hey! Let's do that!" I'd answered.

That conversation had taken place between the two of us almost eight years ago, back in 1985 when Owen retired as the state's conservation warden at Rice Lake.

And as those years passed, when we'd bump into each other at one occasion or another, that talk would be repeated. Only we never quite got around to that fishing trip.

Until a recent day, that is.

A story I wanted to write had pulled Owen and me together once again. And as we finished our business, once more the old words had come out, "Let's go fishing!" This time we would.

Try Long Lake near Birchwood, Owen suggested. Which was fine with me. Long is, as its name implies, a large lake; 3,290 acres of water with 35 miles of shoreline, not counting its islands. It's a lake that's almost in my backyard, yet one I've rarely fished. Not because it's a poor lake. Quite the opposite. It's an excellent producer of big walleyes, northern pike, bass and panfish.

But Long has always been kind of intimidating. It's so big, so complex. I found myself pondering where and how I'd go about learning it. Anderson, on the other hand, knows

"Owen Anderson, about to release a Long Lake Northern Pike"

the lake well, and I welcomed the chance to fish it with him.

Walleye fishing was just beginning to pick up, Dave Kleven said as we launched our boat at Dave's Outboard marina on the west side of the lake. That didn't surprise me, what with our cool, late spring. A lake as large as Long takes time to warm to the point where the walleyes become active.

And with Anderson at the controls, we began a fifteen minute run across the lake, into a long arm of water that extends to the northeast.

"What a day!" Owen remarked as he cut the motor. "We live in the garden spot of the world!" Overhead the morning sun was breaking through a sky of scattered clouds. Out of the north, a whisper of a breeze blew, just cool enough to make my float coat feel good.

And we began our casting, drifting slowly downwind along the densely forested shoreline, verdant green in its late-May foliage.

Three casts, maybe four, and I felt the soft tap of a fish as it picked up my minnow-baited yellow-haired jig. "There's a fish," I said, and set the hook. And in a minute or so, Owen slipped the net under the keeper walleye. One fish in the bag, and we were barely underway.

Onward, along the rocky shore, we drifted. Shortly, Owen was into a fish, a scrappy smallmouth bass. And action for both of us on small northern pike. But no more walleyes.

That became the pattern as the morning passed. Our cloud cover disappeared and the breeze dropped, putting almost a dead calm on the lake. Not good walleye fishing conditions, as the bright sunlight penetrated the water, sending the walleyes deep.

But that's not to say we didn't catch fish. Owen, using all of his guiding know-how, moved us from one place to another, spots where he's had good fishing in the past. And wherever we went, we found the northerns hungry, eager to hammer our lures. With occasional smallmouths mixed in.

We did take one more walleye, a chunky four-pounder that I hooked from a patch of underwater "cabbage" weeds just beginning to grow. A fine fish that added luster to the day.

And through it all, we watched mallards slowly paddling back in the marshes, listened to the honking of Canada geese as they winged past.

We talked...a lot. About old times, and the great people we once worked with, guys like Bill Waggoner, Earle Gingles and Louie Radke.

And about grandchildren. About how one of Owen's, a five-year-old, calls him up and identifies herself as "your fishin' buddy."

It may have taken eight years to get that fishing trip in the other day.

...but it was worth it.

Shedding the Trout Fishing Blues

I've been singing the trout fishing blues lately. Anyone close to me knows that. The reason being that my two favorite streams, Old Dumpy and The Beautiful Lady, have been so riddled with beaver dams that they aren't fun to fish anymore.

I tried. I drove by Old Dumpy, where she crosses a town road, for instance. There she was, sluggish and bloated. I didn't even bother to stop.

And The Beautiful Lady...a priceless stream where I've spent countless hours listening to the music of her rapids, relishing in the tug of her current against my booted legs.

No more. I fished a half mile of her waters a few weeks ago, a half-mile that I've waded, unimpeded, a hundred times. Not now. Five beaver dams now block her flow, creating flowages that inundate marshes, drown balsams, and silence her laughter. I wouldn't go back, I decided. The sight of my old friend's suffering was too much.

So I've been depressed about trout fishing. To the point where I was seriously considering quitting the sport. Maybe I'd bought my last trout stamp. When the fun's gone, why fight it, I figured.

Still, the old feelings continued to stir. Treasured memories of wading a throbbing, vibrant stream, of brook and

"A nice trout catch from a newly-explored stream"

brown trout streaking out from under undercut banks to snatch my lures, of green-headed mallad drakes flushing almost in my face, of golden marsh marigolds and purple violets shining in the sun, and redwing blackbirds calling in the dawn's mist.

Quitting wouldn't be easy.

And a thought crossed my mind. Explore...try some new territory.

And the recollection of a year-old conversation with an old friend came back. A little trout stream twisted and turned through his property. "C'mon out sometime and give it a try!" he'd said.

I parked the truck the other day, slipped into my waders, buckled on my creel. And with fishing rod in hand, walked the trail he'd shown me to the creek. I really didn't know what to expect. I wasn't optimistic. But I'd be fishing for trout again, and without having to tiptoe chest-deep through beaver ponds.

The trail crossed the creek on an old bridge, and I paused. The pool on the downstream side looked inviting. And I picked my way through the tall marsh grass to a shallow sand bar downstream and entered the water. Easing my way back upstream, I positioned myself at the toe of the pool and began my casting.

Perhaps a half-dozen casts, and I felt the solid tug of a fish as it mouthed my nightcrawler-baited hook. A sucker perhaps, I thought and set the hook. Around the pool, the fish swirled. As I brought it to the surface, it's deep yellow color caused me to think it was a bullhead. Another look and I realized it was indeed a trout, a brown trout, deep, chunky and golden, like few I've seen.

A pleasant surprise! And I rebaited, returned to my casting. Five minutes perhaps, and a second fish, obviously larger than the first, a fish that scrapped in wide circles around the pool. And after landing it, I slipped the brilliantly-colored, heavy-bodied, foot-long brook trout into my creel. A special trout, one that sent my spirits soaring.

Upstream, I moved; past the white blooms of dogwood bushes hanging over the water and spires of emerald-green tamaracks etched against the sky. Past deadfalls that created ripples and pools, past deeply-cut banks where the marsh grass hung dense. All likely places for trout to hide.

Fishing a stream for the first time always carries a lot of unknowns. Still the experienced trout fisherman learns to "read" water, little things that instinctively tell him where to place his bait.

And catch fish I did. The stream is listed in DNR's trout regulations as a "black" stream, which means that one can legally take ten fish, no more than five of which can be brown or rainbow trout.

For three hours, I worked my way up that little creek, around its bends, and through its patches of alders. Brook trout were numerous, and I released those hooked lightly, keeping those that weren't. And one more special fish, a second foot-long brookie that swirled at a bank's edge and responded to a cast to that rise.

My walk back to the truck was slow and easy, casual and comfortable, in the lush green grass that carpeted the stream's side. I'd shed the trout fishing blues.

And it felt good.

Spooner Muskie Club

Blue wood smoke wafts its way skyward, lazily drifting before a gentle breeze, disappearing amidst the crowns of the white pines etched against a leaded late-afternoon sky overhead. From a distant secluded bay, the yodel of a loon sounds, its melodious notes floating over the lake too, like the eddying smoke, sifting softly across the pine-shrouded island.

The coals of the campfire burn brightly, oak logs turned grayish-orange, as they radiate their heat upward against the blackened grill. A kettle of beans simmers. A tall coffee pot bubbles. And a layer of chicken parts cook, slowly turning golden brown.

It's shorelunch time.

And the men, members of the Spooner Muskie Club, have gathered once more; as they have for many years, to pursue a sport they love, to socialize, to enjoy the fruits of good fellowship.

There they stand in a loose circle around the fire, dressed in olive drab and camo rain suits and parkas. In little knots they huddle, threes and fours, shaking hands, joshing each other, renewing old acquaintanceships, laughing.

From a wide area, they've come. Doug Morrisette, for instance, is up from Madison. Paul Gottwald's over from

Park Falls. Jerry Rieckhoff's down from Lake Nebagamon; Mike Johnson from Grantsburg.

Sprinkled through the group are youngsters, teenage young men. It's youth day for the club, a fishing outing to which the younger set has been invited. Roger Tollander and his son are there from Webster. And Joe Weiss has a young Spooner friend along. The two young 'uns are having a good time, that's obvious.

For most of the day, the gang's been on the water. They're muskie fishermen, that strange breed of anglers who are willing to fight the odds, who place trying to catch a fish above the actual catching. Therein lies the sport, in the handicapping of oneself. I speak from long experience. I know full well, for example, when I step into my boat for a day of muskie fishing, that my chances of landing a fish are slight.

Still, I go. And sometimes, the gods of fishing fates smile. If not on me, perhaps on a fishing partner. As they had that day.

Dave Zeug and I fished together that recent day. Zeug is DNR's chief conservation warden here in northwest Wisconsin. And he was taking a busman's holiday, so to speak. A day off to fish himself, to partake a bit of the fruits of his labors, the protection of our fish and game.

A recent comer to this area, he'd never fished Big Sisabagama Lake, he'd said. And I'd agreed to show him around, to try to make the right drifts over the lake's rocky bars and weed beds. All to entice a muskie to strike.

Our first action came over a rocky knob that sticks up from the bottom of the lake, a spot where I've raised a number of fish in years past. I'd no sooner got those bragging words out of my mouth, when one decided to grab the black bucktail Dave was casting. Short of the 32-inch limit, the muskie was quickly brought alongside, and with a twist of a pliers, freed of the hook.

A strike early on in a trip is always a good omen, and across the lake we moved to fish a long weedy bar. There again, the fishing gods smiled once more on Zeug.

Our drift had barely begun when "There's one!" Dave exclaimed. A good fish had followed his bait right to the boat, and now he was frantically figure-eighting the bucktail, hoping the fish would strike.

And it did. Now, it's exciting to have a mad three-foot muskie hooked on a six-foot line. For a few moments, Dave was busy there in the bow, his rod bent double, the fish churning the water. Then out it came, leaping almost in his face, to spit the hook.

Downwind we slid, over waving fronds of green underwater vegetation. And another strike for Zeug, this time a cast length from the boat. As every muskie fisherman knows, it's hard to get a good hook "set" under those circumstances. Dave tried, reefing hard on his rod, bringing the muskie swirling to the surface. But then, it was gone, another muskie memory.

Later, on that little pine-covered island, at shorelunch time, we shared that memory and others, as we've done for so many years now.

Along with the chicken, the chowder and the beans...while a loon yodelled in the distance, and the wind sighed in the pinetops up above.

"Tom Newcomb"

A Tribute to Tom Newcomb

"Now the oars of the guideboats are silent..."
The words come from a song in a medley of ballads recently published on tape by Pete and Dorothy Lund of Eagle River. It's a beautiful song, one that tells about the old-time fishing guides that once plied their trade, showing their guests how to catch fish and appreciate nature, here in our North.

And now a guideboat stands empty, over at Boulder Junction...Tommy Newcomb's.

Newcomb died on August 15. A heart attack claimed him suddenly. He was 65.

The church, tucked into the pine woods that surround Boulder Junction, was crowded at the memorial service for Newcomb the other day; his wife, Lola, their four children, the grandchildren, and an outpouring of folks who came to share their grief. And to pay last respects to a man they knew as a good friend.

Up front, resting neatly on a table amongst the bright wreaths of gladiolus, daisies and mums, were some of Newcomb's treasured personal effects. He was a teacher by vocation, and a plaque expressed the appreciation of a girls' basketball team he'd coached to a championship.

And some of his fishing tackle. Two spinning rods, poles

that have caught many a walleye. A wooden showcase tackle box lined with antique River Runts and Bassorenos, for Newcomb was a collector of such lures of the past. Then, a scroll and a plaque certifying his enshrinement into the National Freshwater Fishing Hall of Fame at Hayward as a "Legendary Guide."

And justly so. For Newcomb was a premier guide for fifty years. Born and reared in the Manitowish-Boulder Junction area of Vilas County, he began his guiding when he was barely a teenager. And present at the service were a number of his fellow guides, men who'd worked alongside him over the years.

I had the pleasure of fishing with Tom Newcomb several times, first in 1987 when I joined him and Johnny Walker on the Flambeau Flowage. Walker was a lifelong friend of Newcomb's. The walleyes didn't bite all that well that hot, sunny day. But Newcomb, good guide that he was, cooked a shorelunch that made fishing secondary; potatoes golden in an ancient black skillet, thick steaks broiled over red-hot maple coals, and black coffee served steaming from a tin pot.

And other good times. A journey to Lake Michigan to tie into huge king salmon, to the Ontonagon River in Michigan's upper peninsula for walleyes. And a trip as recent as last April to try the salmon and trout in Lake Superior's Keweenaw Bay.

The most memorable days, however, were those spent at Newcomb's cabin on Island Lake. Seven of us would gather there in November for a last try at the walleyes before winter closed the lake with ice. The weather was usually brutal; cold, snowy, blustery. But, Newcomb once said, "You can't really call yourself a walleye fisherman unless you fish the week before deer season."

There I came to see Tom Newcomb as a fisherman's fisherman. I once wrote that Newcomb could catch walleyes in a gravel pit. And in his boat one morning he once remarked, "I sometimes think I can wish a fish to bite."

But he was more than a good catcher of fish. His years as a guide had polished his style of dealing with people. He was always affable, full of wit, upbeat, even when the fish wouldn't hit and the wind blew fierce, sending snow stinging against our cheeks.

One of the hymns we sang at the service the other day was: "This Is My Father's World." Its words speak to the wonders of the outdoors. When we finished, Pastor Robert Anderson spoke of Tom Newcomb, calling him a friend of Creation and a man of good, reminding us that the word "good" is derived from the word "god."

"They shove out at dawn with hope in their hearts...and return at the sunset's last gleam"...so go the words to the song about the old guides.

There's an empty seat in a guideboat over on Island Lake these days.

There's an emptiness too in the hearts of many of us.

"A last-day-of-the-season catch of Brook and Brown Trout"

A Trout Season Closes

A fishing friend once said to me, "There's no such thing as a bad fishing day." What he meant was that, though things go wrong and the fish don't bite, it's still great to be on the water.

Still, there have been times when my faith in that philosophy has been severely tested. Like recently when I scheduled myself to go trout fishing on the last day of the season. That would be it! The last day! When it'd be over, the season'd be over.

Eagerly, I looked ahead to the day. Forget all the other mish-mosh that creeps into life! Just go fishing! All day!

And the end of September, what a glorious time to be out in the wild. An Indian summer day, I hoped for. One where the air would be crisp, the sky blue, and the sun warm through my beat-up red-and-black wool shirt.

Well, I came close...crisp, blue, sunny, yes! But out of the southwest a gale was blowing, gusts so strong that I had to grab for my hat a couple times, as I trudged in my waders along the trail to one of my favorite trout streams.

Wind! I didn't need that. I knew what laid ahead as I stepped into the water. Try casting a flimsy, spider-web-thin line on a narrow brush-lined trout stream in a crazy cross-wind! And try casting it accurately, which is a fundamental part of successful trout fishing.

It's frustrating. Baits don't go where you want them to. Monofilament line peels off the face of the reel, swirling in tangled messes. Not to mention gusts that strike just as I'm delicately balanced, thigh-deep in cold water, teetering me dangerously close to a frigid dunking.

But fish I would. After all, it was the last day of the season. I'd suffer, and I'd pay the price; all so that hopefully, come February nights, I might dream good dreams about the season.

And things got off to a surprisingly good start, fishing a fairly open pool. Though the wind almost blew my baited hook back in my face a couple times, by timing the blasts, I was able to place my casts fairly well.

One, two, a half dozen, and the gentle tap-tap of a fish mouthing the bait. The hook set told me I was into a respectable trout. Around the pool it raced, fighting deep, putting a good bend in my rod, and finally, tiring, to the surface. A brown, and a nice one. And shortly, I lifted the pound-and-a-halfer from the water. A fine beginning!

Onward, upstream I moved, to where tall marsh grass waved along the water's edge and alders swayed. The wind's effect was obvious. The water's surface was littered with torn twigs and leaves.

Tough fishing, for sure. Yet there's something about a trout stream that grabs me and captures my spirit, even under the worst of conditions. I can lose the world on a mile of good trout water.

Fighting snagged-branches and looped line, I floated my nightcrawler-baited hooks into likely trout hiding places. Shaded, undercut banks. Under debris lodged against overhanging alders. An hour and a couple hundred yards of wading produced only two brook trout worthy of the creel.

But then, from the western horizon, a thick bank of dark clouds began to move across the sky, shielding the bright sun. And the fish began to feed. The wind continued to blow, but a good, or lucky, cast had the promise of a fish.

Ah, those are times of which trout fishing memories are made! Of fish smacking a bait as soon as it hits the water, sometimes so quickly that the hook can't be set. And others that rush pell-mell under the bank's cover, to come out to splash and swirl as I land them.

And one special fish, a beautifully-marked brook trout with red and violet-dotted, gun-barrel-blue sides. A fish more than a foot long, chunky and heavy. A fish that will fuel many a dream come February.

Last, a deep curving bend where the stream flows silent and solemn. There I took my last two fish, hook-jawed male brookies with white-tipped fins.

There, on a sandy spit, with an old jackknife that's seen many a trout trip, I paused to dress my catch, leaving the innards for a hungry mink or raccoon come nightfall.

As I headed up the bank, the wind caught me full blast, sending tears streaming down my cheeks.

Another season was over.

It'd ended with a good day.

Ball Club Lake

The wind blew...and it blew...and it blew!

The trip had been planned as a fishing vacation, with Momma and me joining up with ten other senior citizen couples at Ball Club Lake in northern Minnesota. That's the way it was intended. What it turned into was an outing heavy on vacationing and light on fishing.

Four days we spent at Steve and Karen Prescher's Ball Club Lake Lodge near Deer River. And of those, two days were totally unfishable because of the high winds, and the other two were barely marginal.

We travel U.S. Highway 2 to get to Ball Club. As highways go it's an old-timer, not one of our modern-day four-laner types. And once a person gets a few miles west of Duluth, and away from that city's influence, the old road takes on a nostalgic charm all its own. Look close and one can read a ton of our north-country's history along its flanks.

Through places with colorful names like Floodwood, Swan River, Blackberry, Warba and La Prairie. And of course, Grand Rapids, the granddaddy of them all.

The roadsides are mostly forests now, pine, and aspen and birch, second-growth stands that have regrown since the days of the old-time logging camps and the big forest fires that swept the land. But interspersed are the remnants of the small farms carved from the wilderness by early settlers a century ago.

I look at the sagging old barns, with their fading, flaking red paint, and the small white frame houses, still well-maintained, and I try to read their stories. What tales they could tell! And I find myself tempted to stop for a visit with the folks that live there.

— — — — — — — — — —

Ball Club Lake is a fair-sized body of water, seven miles long and two miles wide. It's a beautiful lake, wild and undeveloped, where bald eagles wing casually past the boat dock and black bears prowl the nearby woods, hoping some careless tourist will leave a bag of garbage goodies out at night.

Our friends come there twice a year. And while the ladies drive into Bemidji and Grand Rapids to cruise the craft shops, the menfolks go fishing.

Perch are our quarry. And when weather conditions are right, the action can be fast. The fish average around ten inches, not real big, but nice filletable size that are excellent on the table. During the two days that Dick Meier, my partner, and I fished, we landed about sixty, while the waves bounced us like corks.

— — — — — — — — — —

Five o'clock is quitting time for the fishing. That's when the boats return to camp and the guys line up, assembly-line fashion, in the fish cleaning house. There on a waist-high counter the fillet knives flash and the water runs as the day's catch is dressed and packaged.

Then comes supper-time, pot luck style. Normally that's outdoors next to the trailers and motor homes of our friends. But this year the weather chased us indoors, into the Lodge's large metal storage building which doubles as a recreation hall, complete with electricity and picnic tables.

There Bill Barton fires up his portable propane gas deep fryer, and while the women are loading the table with hors d'oeuvres, hot dishes, vine-ripened tomatos, cakes and cookies, he drops fresh perch fillets into the sizzling cooking oil. And when the first platter has been filled with Barton's golden nuggets, the line forms and the eatin' begins.

– – – – – – – – – –

The suppers are something to behold as the socializing builds, and the large room echoes with laughter.

And finally, the after-dinner program. Imagine if you will, 22 sixty-something seniors living it up with an old-fashioned sing-a-long, songs like "Let Me Call You Sweetheart" and "You Are My Sunshine, My Only Sunshine!" Songs from another era.

– – – – – – – – – –

And imagine if you will a certain lady belting out a tune she herself had improvised. "Take Me Out To The Mall Game!" it was called.

Her name? Don't ask!

Just guess.

You're right.

"Larry Keith and Dean Volenec fish for Perch on Northern Minnesota's Ball Club Lake"

Mischief's His Game

Dewey's his name, and mischief's his game.

Dewey's a dog, a five-month-old German wire-haired pointer. He's my brother Bill's new huntin' dog, the latest in a string of fine dogs my brother's owned.

I got acquainted with Dewey recently. He's a character, let me tell you.

The call came one evening. My brother was on the line. He was up at his summer cabin east of Mercer, he said. Would I care to come over for a day or two? The walleyes were slow on the lake. But the muskies were kicking up their fins.

So I threw a toothbrush and a set of longjohns into a duffle bag, tossed a couple tackle boxes and three fishing rods in the back of the pickup. And the next morning I headed east, into the rising sun.

"Wow!" I said to myself as I rolled. The fall color was simply spectacular! Highway 70 was ablaze...scarlet oaks, golden maples and aspens, tangerine tamaracks, standing brilliant against a deep blue sky.

Through the Stone Lake country, Couderay, Radisson, and Park Falls, some of my old stompin' ground. And northeast through the Flambeau Flowage boondocks to Mercer. And finally the backroad to Winchester, where my brother's truck was waiting.

Peering out the back window was Dewey, checking out the stranger that'd come to visit.

And in tandem, we drove the last five miles of twisting, gravel trail to the cabin, a place Bill built many years ago, back on a secluded little lake.

He's not alone. He's got neighbors. But the cottages are spaced with taste and judgement, tucked back in the forest of dense second-growth hardwoods, swatched here and there

"Dewey, a five month old German Wire-Haired Pointer"

with patches of somber green balsams and hemlocks. Along the shore, ancient cedars stand. And occasional tall white pines where the eagles and ospreys build bulky nests of sticks high in their tops.

Over it all, hangs an atmosphere of peace and primeval tranquility. We'd be the only people on the lake, what with the neighbors gone for the season. And the silence hanging over the scene was so heavy, one could almost cut it with a knife.

A quick lunch, the boat loaded with gear, and Bill and I shoved off to test our walleye-catching skills.

Dewey'd go along.

Let me tell you about Dewey. Right now, he's mostly skin and bone, growing so fast that his muscles haven't caught up with the rest of him. Across his back is a saddle of chocolate brown fur, offsetting his four legs of brown-ticked white. And his feet! Big! Like he's wearing snowshoes!

And what a face! There it is, a fluffy full beard and a big handle-bar mustache that guard his nose and mouth. Peeking out through massive hairy eyebrows, are two pale-yellow eyes. Expressive eyes, that look at you and seem to say, "Whatcha talkin' about?"

Well, let me tell you, Dewey was all over the boat! A pup at five months I decided was the equivalent of a human youngster at that 'terrible two' stage.

There good 'ol Dew was, chewing on the oar handles, tussling with the anchor rope, tugging at my boot laces. I opened my tackle box, and there was Dew, sniffing its contents.

"Get out of there!" I scolded, fearing he'd come up with the treble hook of a Rapala caught in a nostril.

So up on the seat he came, snuggling tight to my side, against the cold northwest wind that was blowing. And he discovered I had pockets in my float coat, pockets that undoubtedly reek of fully-ripened sandwiches and half-melted candy bars. In went his nose, snuffling and snorting, sampling those delicious smells.

Bill and I didn't catch any fish that afternoon. But getting to know a vibrant young dog was much more fun. Fish we have lots of. But not many young dogs that capture your heart.

Dewey and his master will be off to the cornfields and swales of Iowa come November. There he'll get his first taste of pheasant hunting. I'd like to be there when that first big rooster explodes in front of him, wings clattering, cackling.

The look on his face would be something to see!

An Old Fisherman's Prayer

The Old Fisherman sat on the tailgate of his pickup and slowly slipped on his waders. The last trout fishing trip for the year it would be. Tomorrow the season would close.

He was down a bit; one of those bittersweet, sweet-sour melancholy moods; his thoughts drifting back to the excitement, the anticipation he'd felt a day back in May, when the season had begun.

Slowly he strapped the worn sun-bleached wicker creel to his shoulder; picked up his fishing rod; and stepped into the brushy trail. The old footpath through the woods would take him to a stream, a trout stream.

"The Beautiful Lady," he had long ago named the creek. For over twenty years he'd romanced with her, a love affair that only he understood.

He knew her well; every little quirk, every swing of her personality.

He'd been with her when sunrises peeked rose-colored over low-hanging cloudbanks in the early morning light. Times when he'd heard the first red-winged blackbird call softly back in the willows.

He'd been there with her as the gentle dusk of warm summer evenings settled peacefully over her valley, and the last shafts of afternoon sunshine had filtered through her aspens.

Then, he'd watched the splendor of mighty thunderstorms as they crashed and echoed through the tall white pines; the lightning dancing and flickering, casting ghostly reflections to mirror from her face.

And he'd stood in her waters at the tail of a rapids and listened to her laughter, music more beautiful than any that man could compose.

The Old Fisherman stepped into the stream and began his casts. Slowly, cautiously, like a blue heron stalking its prey, his booted feet reading the bottom, he worked his way.

He'd passed that way many times. And he knew exactly where to position himself to make his casts, a thick file of memories in his brain of fish caught, of mistakes made, telling him.

Up through the spruce tree hole, his favorite, where he once took a twenty-two inch brown trout. There he'd stood motionless in waist-deep water once and had a red fox trot past him on the bank so close that the whiskers on its nose could be counted.

Then through the riffles where the velvet-antlered buck deer in its red summer coat had slipped like a phantom from the marsh grass to dip its muzzle for a drink.

On to the pool below the old logging dam where The Beautiful Lady's water swirled deep, eddying in dark circles. Where the hen wood ducks and mallards skitter, faking their broken wings while their fluffy offspring flit like downy waterbugs into the weeds.

Methodically, the Old Fisherman moved up the stream, fishing old memories, landing a brown trout here, a brookie there. The fish didn't really matter. Being there with his Beautiful Lady was all that did.

On past the run where a mink had slithered with fluid

motion through the roots of the alders one morning. Over the fallen dead elm tree the red squirrels use for a bridge; skidaddling across, their tails held high. Through the marsh where the little doe had bounded suddenly out of the willows to splash not ten feet in front of him. Past the sunken log where one night he'd tripped, fallen forward, filled his waders with cold water. And almost lost his prized pipe.

And last, the sharp bend where the Lady's waters cut deep against a rocky ledge; where he'd leave her once more.

The old man unbuckled his creel, laid it on the mossy bank. With an ancient jack knife, he dressed his catch; a ritual always performed in that same exact place.

Finished, he loaded and lit his pipe and watched its blue smoke hang in the evening air. The Beautiful Lady pushed and gurgled, gently caressing his boots as he rested.

Back in the woods; a deer, catching the scent of his pipe, whistled in alarm. A scarlet maple leaf drifted lazily past on the current.

And he said his little prayer.

"Lord, if you call...please...let me bring just a quarter mile of her along."